FIONA BECKETT'S
CHEESE COURSE

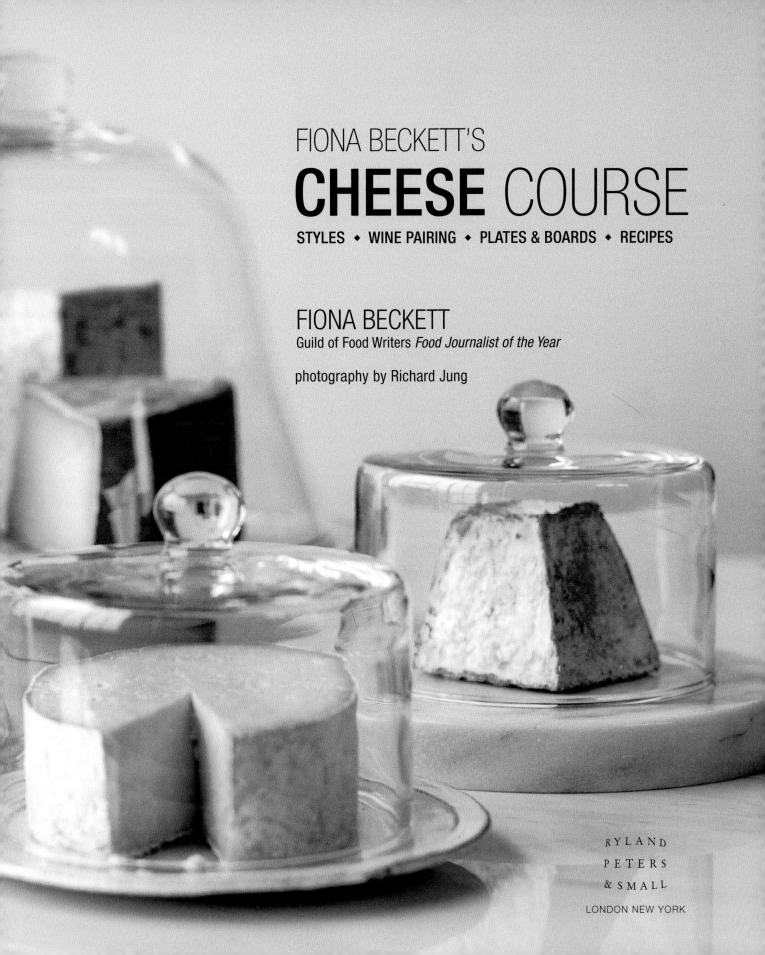

FIONA BECKETT'S
CHEESE COURSE

STYLES ◆ WINE PAIRING ◆ PLATES & BOARDS ◆ RECIPES

FIONA BECKETT
Guild of Food Writers *Food Journalist of the Year*

photography by Richard Jung

RYLAND
PETERS
& SMALL
LONDON NEW YORK

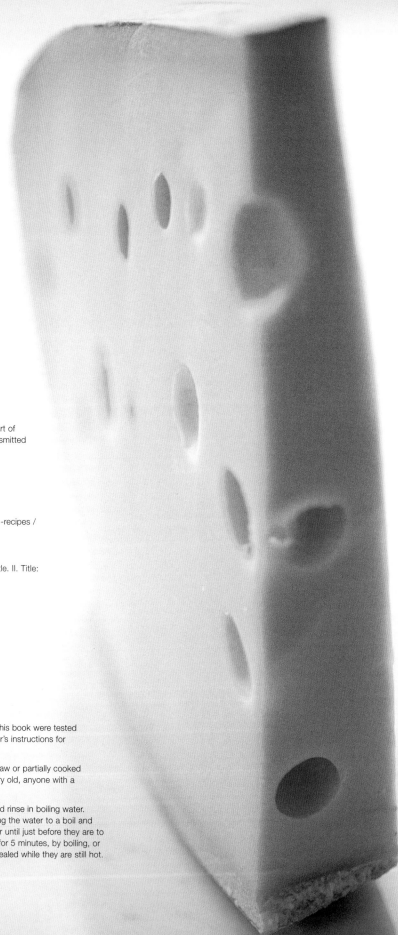

Author's Acknowledgments

Many thanks to the cheese makers and cheese shops who
have shared their knowledge and time, especially Ruaridh
Buchanan of Paxton & Whitfield, who also supplied many
of the cheeses for my tastings. Also to James Rackam of
Emporia for providing some fascinating drinks and liqueurs
for my pairing experiments, and my brilliant team at Ryland
Peters & Small—commissioning editor Alison Starling,
editor Céline Hughes, designer and fellow cheese
obsessive Steve Painter, and photographer Richard Jung.

**Design, Photographic Art Direction,
   and Prop Styling** Steve Painter
Senior Editor Celine Hughes
Production Controller Toby Marshall
Art Director Leslie Harrington
Publishing Director Alison Starling

Food Stylist Linda Tubby
Indexer Penelope Kent

First published in the US in 2009
by Ryland Peters & Small, Inc.
519 Broadway, 5th Floor
New York, NY 10012
www.rylandpeters.com

10 9 8 7 6 5 4 3

Text © Fiona Beckett 2009
Design and photographs © Ryland Peters & Small 2009

ISBN 978 1 84597 917 1

Library of Congress Cataloging-in-Publication Data

Beckett, Fiona.
   Fiona Beckett's cheese course : styles--wine pairing--plates & boards--recipes /
Fiona Beckett ; photography by Richard Jung.
      p. cm.
   Includes bibliographical references and index.
   ISBN 978-1-84597-917-1 (alk. paper)
   1. Cheese--Varieties. 2. Wine and wine making. 3. Entertaining. I. Title. II. Title:
Cheese course.
   SF271.B44 2009
   641.3'735--dc22
                                        2009023595

Printed and bound in China

 For digital editions visit
rylandpeters.com/apps.php

Notes

• All spoon measurements are level, unless otherwise specified.

• Ovens should be preheated to the specified temperature. Recipes in this book were tested
using a regular oven. If using a convection oven, follow the manufacturer's instructions for
adjusting temperatures.

• All eggs are medium, unless otherwise specified. Recipes containing raw or partially cooked
egg, or raw fish or shellfish, should not be served to the very young, very old, anyone with a
compromised immune system or pregnant women.

• Sterilize preserving jars before use. Wash them in hot, soapy water and rinse in boiling water.
Place in a large saucepan and cover with hot water. With the lid on, bring the water to a boil and
boil for 15 minutes. Turn off the heat, then leave the jars in the hot water until just before they are to
be filled. Invert the jars onto clean paper towels to dry. Sterilize the lids for 5 minutes, by boiling, or
according to the manufacturer's instructions. Jars should be filled and sealed while they are still hot.

CONTENTS

INTRODUCTION

If I was forced to choose just one food to eat for the rest of my life, it would have to be cheese. Not a day goes by when I don't sneak a nibble from the fridge, not a week when I don't make a cheese-based recipe. There's such an incredible variety of different cheeses—more than 1,000 in France alone—that I don't think I could ever become bored with it or fail to find an interesting new one to try.

And that's the problem for most people. So much choice, so much to learn. What on earth do you buy and how do you serve it, let alone find a wine to drink with it? These days, one's simply spoilt for choice.

This book is all about introducing you to cheese and styles of cheese you might not be familiar with, and helping you to enjoy them more. Discover how cheese is made and why it varies so much; how to create the perfect classic cheese board or a stylish, modern one with a twist; how to entertain with cheese (reinvent the wine and cheese party!), borrowing ideas from all round the world; how to introduce it into a romantic dinner for two or make it the focus of a barbecue or a brunch.

There's advice about how to pick the perfect wine for different types of cheeses (you'll find that white wine and sweet wines are a revelation), as well as other drinks, such as sherry, beer, hard cider, and whisky—and even tea! You'll learn which breads are the best partners for different cheeses, and which crackers. And finally, you'll get some ideas on how to make the ultimate cheese sandwich.

There are cheese ideas to match your mood and the season. Light, refreshing cheese plates for spring, vividly fruity ones for summer, mellow ones for fall, and glowingly warm ones for winter, including ideas for some show-stopping Thanksgiving and Christmas cheese boards.

There are recipes—mmmm, some really good recipes though I say so myself. If you're a mac and cheese fan, you've got to try the Extra-crispy Macaroni and Cheese (read the recipe on page 120 for the secret). There's my favorite new fondue made from hard cider and farmstead cheeses; an Irresistible Italian Four-cheese Pizza; and a tempting Tartiflette, the wickedly indulgent Alpine potato and cheese dish, a must for après-ski eating. Not to mention a couple of mouthwatering cheesecakes and some easy Raspberry and Ricotta Hotcakes and Double Cheese and Bacon Muffins to get your day off to the perfect start.

And then there's the basic tips you need to know: how to pick a cheese in perfect condition and how to make sure it stays that way. How to cut it, what to cut it with, and how to use up the leftovers. And finally some new ideas for enjoying cheese without piling on the pounds—essential for all us cheese addicts!

I have to confess I have absolutely loved working on this book, which, thanks to designer Steve Painter and photographer Richard Jung, looks more beautiful than I could ever have imagined. I hope you enjoy reading and cooking from it as much as I enjoyed writing it.

LEFT *Selection of goat cheeses*

THE WONDERFUL WORLD OF CHEESE

THIS PAGE *Wedges of Brie*
LEFT *(Top and back) Isle of Mull, (bottom) Appleby's Cheshire*

WHAT MAKES CHEESE TASTE SO DIFFERENT?

It's one of the miracles of cheese that one ingredient—milk—can be turned into so many different varieties of cheese. You really wouldn't believe it walking into the average cheese shop with its myriad different shapes, sizes, and colors—or when you look at the line-up on a cheese board.

The process of making cheese can be incredibly simple but also highly skilled and labor-intensive. Many recipes are ancient ones going back several centuries. To make a good cheese, never mind a great one, you need to have had years of experience. And to taste the best cheeses in the world is like tasting a fine wine.

There are many variables, some of which are highly technical, but, keeping it simple, the most influential factors are the quality of the milk, the recipe the cheese is made from, and how and for how long the cheese is matured.

HOW CHEESE IS MADE

At its most basic, the process of making cheese couldn't be easier. You simply separate the solids in milk (the curds) from the liquid (whey) as you do in a simple recipe for labneh (see page 140). Of course, there's more to it than that otherwise all cheeses would have the same taste and texture. Some are simply molded, others are pressed, some are heat-treated, some have bacteria introduced to turn them blue, some have rinds that develop naturally, others are washed or rubbed. Think of it like a whole lot of different recipes.

The easiest way I find to understand the process is to follow a single cheese through from start to finish as I did when I visited Keen's in south-west England. Keen's is a traditional producer of **West Country Farmhouse Cheddar**, a style of cheese that has its own Protected Designation of Origin (PDO). It's also one of only three cheeses which is entitled to be called "Somerset Artisan Cheddar."

The milk, which is unpasteurized, comes from Keen's own herd of Friesian cows. First they introduce a starter culture which sours the milk and kicks off the process of separating it into curds and whey. They source this from a laboratory that supplies cultures based on local microflora, to preserve the unique character of their cheese. Then rennet, an enzyme extracted from calves' stomachs, is added, again to accelerate the production of curds [1] [2]. (Vegetarian cheeses use other coagulants—see page 152.)

The milk goes through successive heating processes as each ingredient is added, finally forming a soft, sloppy mass called "junket" which is chopped up to extract more liquid. Other softer cheeses are formed at this point but Cheddar goes through a unique process called cheddaring, which is fascinating to watch. The curds—by this stage a mass of buttercup-yellow granules—are pulled to the side of a large trough [3] to drain off the watery whey. As they're cut and re-cut [4], stacked and re-stacked [5], the texture changes, becoming firm and elastic. The weight of the layers pushes the blocks of cheese down, thereby extracting the rest of the whey [6].

When the cheddaring process is complete, the curd is passed through a mill to cut it into smaller, even-size pieces. Salt—another crucial ingredient—is added to stabilize the curd, develop the flavor, and to stop bacteria growing.

Then the cheese is put into molds and left to drain [7] [8] [9]. Finally, the cheeses are smeared with lard [10] and triple-wrapped in cheesecloth [11], a permeable coating that allows air to get to the cheese and moisture to continue to evaporate.

As the cheese ages, the surface gradually becomes colonized by molds. The "truckles," as the huge cheeses are called, are regularly turned and rubbed to ensure they mature evenly. You can see the rinds evolve from the multi-colored spots on a cheese that is a few weeks old to the grayish, craggy surface of a mature one [12]. Most of Keen's Cheddars are stored for about 10–12 months, although they do age them for up to 2 years (see more on maturing cheese overleaf).

So what exactly makes other cheeses taste so different?

OTHER WAYS OF MAKING CHEESE

There are many variations in the way that milk is handled that will result in different cheeses.
◆ Cheese makers may use different starter cultures to kick off the cheesemaking process or introduce bacteria that will create a certain type of

rind, texture, or flavor, as with bloomy-rinded cheese, such as **Brie**, cheese with holes, such as **Emmental**, and blues, such as **Stilton**.

◆ The amount the curds are stirred and the size they are cut will influence the final cheese—the more vigorous the stirring, the smaller the particles and the harder the cheese.

◆ Some cheeses are subject to higher temperatures or more heat processes than others. With **Mozzarella** and **Provolone**, the curds are left in hot water for some hours, then stretched or pulled into shape (a style known as "stretched curd" or *pasta filata*).

◆ Cheeses are placed in different-shaped molds (sometimes baskets) and may or may not be pressed. The longer a cheese is pressed and the greater the

pressure, the more moisture is extracted and the harder the resulting cheese will be. Semisoft and blue cheeses are not pressed.

◆ Salt can be added in different ways—as a brine, as in **Parmesan**, or directly on to the curds, as in **Cheddar**.

◆ A blue cheese will be pierced with needles to allow the characteristic blue veins to spread through the cheese.

◆ The rind may develop in different ways. Washed-rind cheeses, for example, may be rubbed with a brine solution or alcohol, such as wine, cider, or marc (see page 18). White-rinded cheeses, such as **Brie**, can be sprayed to develop their characteristic white, velvety surface.

THE MILK

Given that cheese consists of one main ingredient, the character of the milk used is paramount and will vary from animal to animal, breed to breed, from one pasture to another, from winter to summer, and from morning to evening.

THE ANIMAL

Many animals produce milk for cheese we never get to taste—camel, reindeer, and yak among them—but the most common are cows, goats, and sheep. In general, cow's milk tends to be the richest in color with a creamy, buttery taste; sheep's milk is more concentrated and tangy; goat's milk is fresher tasting and more citrussy. Cow's milk tends to make richer-colored cheeses, while goat's and sheep's cheeses, which are more common across southern Europe and the Eastern Mediterranean, are a purer white or ivory color. There are also variations between breeds. Jersey and Guernsey cows' milk, for example, is particularly rich and yellow.

At one time, you used to be able to say definitively that a certain style of cheese came from a certain type of animal but since cheese makers have become more experimental, there's a much greater crossover of styles, with Camembert-type cheeses being made from goat's milk, for example, or blues made from buffalo milk.

THE PASTURE

The quality of the milk will also depend on the pasture the animal is grazing on —whether it is lush green grass, alpine, flower-filled mountain pastures, or desolate scrub. In some cases you can actually pick up the flavor of herbs or of salt from animals which have grazed on pastures near the sea. You sometimes find the same flavors in cheese and wine from the same area. Both **Sancerre** and a **Crottin de Chavignol** share a mineral flavor, for example.

At some times of year the animals won't be out to pasture at all and will be eating hay and other winter rations, which will make their cheese less full-flavored and aromatic.

The process of moving livestock from one type of pasture to another, from the valleys to the mountains, is called transhumance. That can be reflected in the name of the cheese. For example, there are different versions of **Beaufort**, called **Beaufort d'été** (summer Beaufort) and **Beaufort d'Alpage**, which is made in mountain chalets by the herdsmen who look after the cows.

THE TIME OF YEAR

As just noted and rarely realized, cheese is seasonal and also—increasingly important with today's bizarre variations in climate—affected by the weather. Even in the spring or summer, a traditionally productive time for cattle and other milk-producing animals, an unseasonal cold snap or a storm can affect the yield. Artisanal cheese—handmade cheese made on a farm or by a small producer from locally sourced milk—isn't a standard product.

In general, soft cheeses like goat cheese are at their best in the spring; semisoft cheeses, such as **Brie** and **Camembert**, in the summer; and hard cheeses, such as **Cheddar** and **Stilton**, which mature for several months, in the winter. Some cheeses, such as **Vacherin Mont d'Or**, are only available at certain times of year—in this specific case from October to March. Others like **Gouda**, **Comté**, or **Parmesan**, which are often matured for more than 18 months, show little seasonal variation.

WHETHER THE MILK IS PASTEURIZED

The big issue in cheese making is whether milk should be pasteurized (heat-treated) or not. Large companies do it routinely to avoid any risk of contamination. Artisanal cheese makers tend to avoid it on the basis that it inhibits the individual character of their cheese, a view echoed by many ardent cheese lovers. In the end, it's a question of personal preference, although certain individuals, especially pregnant women and the elderly, are advised not to take the risk of eating untreated cheese (see page 152).

MATURING CHEESE

You'd think the most important person so far as any cheese was concerned was the cheese maker. Well, surprisingly not! Equally, if not more important, is the role of the *affineur*, the person who matures the cheeses and ensures they reach the point of sale—store counter

or restaurant—in perfect condition. The cheese maker and *affineur* may, of course, be one and the same person, and in the case of younger cheeses which don't hang around for more than a few weeks, often are. But more usually *affineurs* are attached to a cheese shop or, occasionally, to a restaurant (Max McCalman of Artisanal in New York and Christophe Demeyer of The Greenhouse in London being good examples). And in some cases where extended ageing of cheeses is the norm, as in a **Parmigiano-Reggiano** (**Parmesan**) or **Grana Padano** factory, there may be a whole team of *affineurs*.

Just like a cellar-master, they care for each cheese individually, turning it, brushing or washing its rind, and checking its interior in the case of bigger cheeses until they decide the optimum moment has been reached to sell them. Some customers will want their cheeses more mature than others, just as some prefer their wines or steak aged for longer. The *affineurs* must make sure in the process that the cheeses don't dry out or attract the wrong kind of mold (artisanal Cheddar, for example, can develop veins like a blue cheese—fine for aficionados, but regarded with suspicion by the uninitiated).

Nowadays this process generally takes place in pristine storage rooms with laboratories on hand where the temperature and humidity are precisely controlled. When I visited one of France's most famous *affineurs*, Bernard Antony, who supplies cheese to many of France's top Michelin-starred restaurants, I was impressed by the fact that you could barely detect the smell of cheese but that each cheese was nonetheless full of character. Like other top *affineurs*, Bernard and his son Jean-Francois are most particular about the producers

they work with and select only those cheeses that meet their requirements.

HOW LONG CAN CHEESE AGE?

In general, cheeses are aged for weeks or months rather than years but there are a few, such as **Parmigiano-Reggiano**, **Oude Gouda**, and **Vieux Mimolette**, that can be aged for a good deal longer. In the main, these are large cheeses, as smaller cheeses would dry out too quickly.

What happens as cheese ages is that it loses moisture, concentrating the flavor. This generally makes them easier to match with wine, especially red wine, than younger, hard cheeses, as they don't tend to have as many volatile aromas and flavors. They also have the advantage of keeping better under domestic storage conditions than younger cheeses so you can store them for several weeks—if they last that long!

WHY IS CHEESE SO EXPENSIVE?

It sometimes comes as a shock when I get presented with the bill in a cheese shop. After all, milk is not an expensive ingredient. However, it takes a surprising amount of milk to make a good-quality cheese—roughly ten times as much as the weight of the finished cheese. A **Beaufort** of 88–100 lbs., for example, will need about 525 quarts of milk (around 130 gallons). It could take one cow around 10–12 days to produce that. Add to that the weeks and months of care and attention that goes into the cheese-maturing process and the long distances that many rare artisanal cheeses have to travel and you can see how the cost adds up. The only upside is that expensive cheeses tend to be more intensely flavored so that you need to eat slightly less of them!

THE DIFFERENT STYLES OF CHEESE: YOUNG UNRINDED CHEESES

There are a number of ways of categorizing cheese, some of them involving descriptions that are understood by producers and specialist cheese shops but are obscure to us, the public. What's the difference between a **semisoft** and a **semihard** cheese, for example, or between a **natural-rind** and a **washed-rind** cheese? It is confusing. In my view the consistency of a cheese and the presence or absence of rind is the easiest way to look at cheese, together with how strong the flavor is.

TASTE AND COMPARE

When you next go to the farmers' market, buy a goat cheese at three different stages: a couple of days old, a week or 10 days old, and a month old. Taste and see the difference!

Young, unrinded cheeses are a popular style dominated by goat and sheep's cheeses. When they're first made, they're light and moussey, just formed into a small flat disk or cylinder. A few days on they can be crumbled and a week or so later sliced. After a month they will have acquired a protective grayish coating of mold, often described as a "natural rind." Sometimes they're rolled in fresh herbs or ash.

Many first-time cheese makers and stallholders make these sorts of cheeses so there are a great many that are unnamed or named simply after the farm where they're made. Two better-known ones are the pyramid-shaped **Valençay**, **Capriole Farm goat cheeses** from Indiana, and **Cypress Grove's Humboldt Fog**.

Another well-known example is **Mozzarella**, which is heat-treated to create its characteristic springy, stretchy texture. It is known as a *pasta filata* (stretched curd) cheese in Italy (see page 12). Most Mozzarella these days is made from cow's milk though the most prized artisanal Mozzarella cheeses are made from the milk of water buffalo.

The by-product of Mozzarella is **ricotta**, which is made from the drained-off whey. It's one of a number of light soft cheeses that can be used both in sweet and savory dishes. Others include **fromage frais** (otherwise known as **fromage blanc**), **quark**, and the Greek cheese **Manouri**. Richer examples are **cream cheese** and **mascarpone**, which is used for the celebrated Italian dessert tiramisù. You can see what a straightforward process making a soft cheese is if you look at the recipes for labneh on page 140.

SALTED CHEESES

Salted or brined cheeses, such as **Feta** share the characteristics of a young cheese, being crumbly and unrinded, but are often aged, at least in the best artisanal examples. The brine in which they are stored not only protects them from the air, which means they don't develop a protective crust or mold, but also gives them their characteristic salty taste. They are traditionally made from a mixture of different milks, usually sheep's and goat's milks.

Clockwise from top left: ricotta, young button of goat cheese, Perroche, fromage frais, buffalo Mozzarella

Taste the difference between a creamy Brie de Meaux and an artisanal Camembert.

BRIE- AND CAMEMBERT-STYLE CHEESES

Technically, the term for this style of cheese is "bloomy-rinded," referring to the downy white surface that these cheeses acquire as they mature. The effect is induced by the introduction of a mold called *penicillium candidum,* which protects the surface of the cheese from other molds.

Unlike other cheeses, Brie and Camembert, which are also known as semisoft cheeses, get softer and more voluptuous as they age rather than firmer and drier. When young they can be quite bland and chalky but as time goes on the center develops a more unctuous creamy texture that can have a marked flavor of mushrooms. Except in very well matured cheeses, the rind remains quite palatable, adding a nutty flavor to each mouthful. As with other cheeses, unpasteurized versions tend to have a stronger flavor, Camembert generally being rather stronger than Brie. The best have the name of a region or town appended to them, for example **Camembert de Normandie**, **Brie de Meaux**, **Brie de Melun**, and so on. Brie is generally made in much bigger wheels than Camembert.

Traditionally this style of cheese was made with cow's milk but many modern cheese makers, particularly in the US, are making them with goat's milk. Good examples are the **Hudson Valley Camemberts** produced by the Old Chatham Sheepherding Company.

There are also white-rinded cheeses which are made to a slightly different recipe and in a different shape, such as **Gaperon** from the Auvergne, which is flavored with garlic and peppercorns so it could be classified as a flavored cheese (see page 25).

Pregnant women are advised not to eat bloomy-rinded cheeses because of the risk of listeria (see page 152).

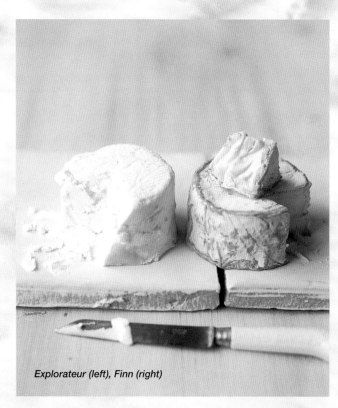

Explorateur (left), Finn (right)

ULTRA-CREAMY CHEESES

Some bloomy-rinded cheeses are exceptionally rich and creamy thanks to the addition of cream during the cheesemaking process. Referred to as double- and triple-crème cheeses, it's a style that's popular in France, which produces some of the most indulgent examples—**Explorateur**, **Brillat-Savarin**, and **Pierre Robert** among them. **Finn** is a British cheese made in this style.

A FRAGILE FLAVOR

Once cheeses of this style have become mature, they deteriorate quite rapidly. The rind becomes progressively softer and stickier, acquiring a slightly ammoniac aroma and flavor that only hardcore cheese lovers will appreciate. If you buy an artisanal Camembert or Brie in perfect condition from a specialist cheese shop, it's better to eat it the same day, ideally picking it up at the last minute and keeping it in a cool place rather than in the refrigerator (though obviously don't leave it out for hours).

WASHED-RIND AND SEMISOFT CHEESES

This category covers a wide range of cheeses that can range from mild to extremely pungent in flavor. And indeed one single cheese can cover that spectrum depending how long it is matured. A young Taleggio, for example, a washed-rind cheese from Lombardy in Italy, can be quite mild but an unpasteurized version can be overpowering if you're unused to it.

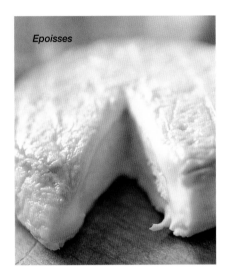

Epoisses

TASTE AND COMPARE

Try washed-rind cheeses from different countries, e.g. French Munster or Epoisses, an English Stinking Bishop, and an Irish Ardrahan. Or compare—if you dare—a relatively mild washed-rind cheese, such as Morbier with a really stinky one, such as Epoisses or Langres.

Many washed-rind cheeses were first developed in the monasteries. They are described as "washed-rind" because the surface of the cheese is rubbed with a brine solution which promotes the growth of a bacterium. This breaks down the texture of the cheese, turning it soft and pliable rather than firm. (These cheeses are usually unpressed.)

It also develops their characteristic farmyardy aroma, sticky rind, and rich array of colors, which range from sunset pink to deep orange. Beer, cider, and marc (a distillate of grape skins and pips) can also be used to wash cheese. Well-known examples are **Epoisses**, **Langres**, **Munster**, and **Reblochon** from France, **Chimay** from Belgium (produced by the brewery), **Appenzeller** from Switzerland, and **Stinking Bishop** from Gloucestershire in England. There are also some fine Irish washed-rind cheeses including **Ardrahan**, **Durrus**, and **Gubbeen**. **Cowgirl Creamery's Red Hawk** is one of the best in the US.

The "bark" of washed-rind cheeses tends to be worse than their "bite." They may smell stinky but the taste is usually milder than you'd imagine. Typically they have a pliable, slightly springy "paste" (what you usually call the center of a cheese), which can be quite sweet and nutty in flavor. They are surprisingly good in cooking, giving a rich, full taste to recipes (see Tartiflette on page 112).

SEMISOFT CHEESES

There are also semisoft cheeses which are not washed. They share washed-rind cheeses' supple texture but don't have their pungent aroma. Examples are **Saint-Nectaire** and **Tomme de Savoie** (and similar French tomme or Italian toma-style cheeses).

Probably the ultimate washed-rind cheese so far as connoisseurs are concerned, **Vacherin Mont d'Or** is

OPPOSITE *Ardrahan (left), Durrus (right)*

a seasonal cheese only available from October to March. It doesn't have its fellow cheeses' pungency but makes up for it with a luxuriant, voluptuous texture that is accentuated by baking it in its box.

Confusingly, the French and the Swiss both lay claim to Vacherin, which is made to a similar recipe on both sides of the Alps. Despite the fact that the cheese appears to have been invented in France, the Swiss are entitled (much to the annoyance of the French) to use the name **Vacherin Mont D'Or** on their boxes. The French version is simply called **Mont D'Or** or, less commonly, **Vacherin du Haut-Doubs**.

Vacherin Mont D'Or

TASTE AND COMPARE

Compare a Beaufort (pictured, center) or Comté with a mature farmstead Cheddar, such as Keen's
(pictured, left) and a Manchego (pictured, right). This is a nice little cheese board, come to think of it.
You could also compare three different wines with it: a Savoie white, the traditional accompaniment
for a Beaufort, a St Emilion with the Cheddar, and a Rioja Reserva with the Manchego.

HARD CHEESES

How hard is a hard cheese? Some experts consider only rock-hard crystalline cheeses, such as Parmesan, to be truly hard but most of us would include semihard cheeses, such as Cheddar or Gruyère.

What cheeses made in this style tend to have in common is a process that involves cutting and heating the curds and pressing the just-formed cheese in order to expel as much of the whey as possible. They are hard in the sense that they contain less liquid than other cheeses, and firm as opposed to soft or pliable.

Isle Of Mull

As well as being pressed, hard cheeses may also be dipped in a brine solution to harden the rind (though not to promote bacteria as in a washed-rind cheese) and are generally aged for longer than other cheeses—in some cases for up to four years.

As with other styles of cheese, their taste and texture will depend on how long they are matured. A young **Cheddar** or **Gouda**, for example, will be milder and more pliable than an older one from which still more moisture has evaporated and which will have much more depth of flavor.

These are the main types of cheeses that fall into this category.

WAXY SWISS-STYLE AND DUTCH-STYLE CHEESES

These include French and Swiss cow's milk cheeses, such as **Gruyère** (Swiss), **Beaufort**, and **Comté** (both French). They have an ivory to yellow color (depending on the season), a smooth, waxy texture, and a hard rind. Although they are sometimes rubbed with a brine solution, the flavor is sweet and nutty

without the farmyardy elements of a washed-rind cheese or the "bite" of a mature Cheddar. Aged versions of these cheeses, such as **Vieux Comté** and **Vieux Gruyère d'Alpage**, are some of the best the cheese world has to offer. Gouda-style cheeses, such as **Gouda** itself, **Coolea** from Ireland and **Winchester Gouda** from California also fit into this category, although they have a deeper color and age in a different way, becoming more crystalline in texture. **Oude Gouda** can become almost as crumbly as **Parmigiano-Reggiano** (see below).

CHEDDAR AND OTHER BRITISH TERRITORIAL CHEESES

Again there's variation within this group, from mild **Cheshire** and **Wensleydale** cheeses with their slightly crumbly texture to the powerful taste and firmer consistency of an authentic farmstead **Cheddar**. Although Cheddar is made all over the world, the original cheese comes from Somerset and is made by a unique process which involves stacking the blocks of curd so that moisture is

squeezed out, wrapping the cheese in cheesecloth, pressing it, and ageing it in huge truckles (see pages 10–11).

HARD SHEEP'S CHEESES

Just as goat cheeses dominate the soft cheese category, so there are many sheep's cheeses in this section. Some are "semihard," such as **Berkswell** from England, Spanish **Manchego**, and **Ossau-Iraty** from the south-west of France. Some are harder and more crumbly, such as Italian **Pecorino**. They tend to be tangier, less creamy, and more obviously salty than cow's cheese.

VERY HARD CHEESES

These are the oldest cheeses you're likely to come across—cheeses that are so hard they have become almost crystalline and need to be shaved or grated rather than sliced. The best-known type by far is **Parmesan** or **Parmigiano-Reggiano**, but matured **Grana Padano** and **Pecorino** (also from Italy), **Sbrinz** from Switzerland, **Roomano** from Holland, and **Vella Dry Jack** from California are similar in style.

BLUE CHEESES

Some people shy off blue cheeses because they taste too strong but, as with other types of cheese, there is a wide range of flavors and textures.

Blue cheeses develop their characteristic blue veining when a harmless penicillin mold is added to the milk or curds. Once the cheese is formed, fine steel needles are inserted to expose the center to oxygen, which enables the mold to spread throughout the cheese. Some cheeses are much bluer than others: a Cambozola or blue Brie, for example, will have very little veining, whereas the Spanish Cabrales is covered with blue streaks (see picture opposite, top right, which compares it with the barely blue Caradon Blue). In general, the greater the number of veins, the stronger the flavor.

Most blue cheeses are unpressed so are quite soft or crumbly in texture and fall into one of three groups.

MILDER BLUES

The best-known cheeses that meet this description are blue Bries, such as **Cambozola** and **Gorgonzola dolce** (or **Dolcelatte** as it's also called). Although there is a touch of the characteristic saltiness and bitterness of blue cheese, this is offset by the creamy texture. There is, however, a trend towards milder blue cheeses with slightly more character, which has seen the introduction of interesting new blues like **Barkham Blue** (winner of many awards in the last six years), **Caradon Blue** and **Point Reyes Original Blue**.

MELLOW BLUES

The outstanding cheese in this style is undoubtedly **Stilton**, not only the most famous English blue but arguably the most famous English cheese after Cheddar. It is also one of the few to have a Protected Designation of Origin (PDO)—it can only be produced in the counties of Derbyshire, Leicestershire, and Nottinghamshire. Some "extra-matured" Stiltons pack quite a punch but in general this is a mellow, rich-tasting blue protected by its characteristic crumbly gray rind. Good producers are Colston Bassett and Cropwell Bishop. Since all Stiltons are now made from pasteurized milk, a new unpasteurized blue has come on the market called **Stichelton**, which tastes like Stiltons used to taste. Other comparable blues are the striking orange **Shropshire Blue**, **Rogue River Blue** from Oregon, and **Fourme D'Ambert** from France.

STRONG BLUES

This group includes the world's other best-known blues: **Gorgonzola** from Lombardy and **Roquefort**, the famous sheep's milk cheese from southern France—both are quite distinctive. **Gorgonzola**, though strong (or "piccante") is rich and creamy, good for melting into pasta or risotto (see picture opposite, top left, comparing smooth, creamy **Gorgonzola** with mellow, crumbly **Stilton**). **Roquefort** is much sharper and saltier, a perfect partner to the equally famous sweet wine Sauternes. The Spanish also have a number of distinguished strong blues, such as **Cabrales** and **Valdeón**.

CHEESE TIP

If you find a particular blue cheese too strong, you can always mix it with a little soft butter or cream to make a milder cheese spread and spread it on crackers as a little canapé to serve with drinks. Alternatively, mix it with other cheeses in a pasta bake or quiche.

TASTE AND COMPARE

It's fascinating to compare the taste and texture of the world's best blues, so do try a Stilton, a Gorgonzola, and a Roquefort together. Explore some blues you haven't tried, such as a Barkham Blue, a Bleu d'Auvergne, and a Cabrales. Or take a look at the difference between a similar cheese made with different milks—Cashel Blue (cow's milk) and Crozier Blue (sheep's milk).

Stilton and Gorgonzola

Cabrales and Caradon Blue

Cashel Blue

Barkham Blue

Clockwise from top: Gouda with wild garlic, Gaperon with garlic and pepper, Banon

FLAVORED CHEESES

There are a remarkable number of flavored cheeses nowadays. Many are disapproved of by cheese cognoscenti but flavoring cheese has perfectly respectable antecedents.

Adding flavoring ingredients tends to be done to add visual interest and flavor to younger cheeses, although there are a few harder examples, such as **Majorero Pimentón**, a goat cheese from the Canary Islands where the flavor (in this case pimentón or paprika) is rubbed into the rind. (Washed-rind cheeses are in effect flavored by the type of alcohol that's rubbed into them but they tend not to be categorized by that flavor.)

Some, like the French cheese **Gaperon**, contain the flavors within the cheese, in this case garlic and peppercorns. Some cheeses, such as **Gouda** with cumin seeds, contain spices, others chiles, yet others herbs, such as sage or chives. There are also cheeses—which I have to admit I am less keen on—flavored with fruits like apricots or cranberries, and even chocolate if you look hard enough.

Other cheeses, such as the British goat cheese **Perroche** or the Corsican **Fleur du Maquis**, are rolled or coated with fresh or dried herbs or with spices, such as peppercorns. There is even one, **Hereford Hop**, which is rolled in toasted hops.

Still others get their flavor from the leaves in which they're wrapped. The Provençal cheese **Banon**, for example, is wrapped in chestnut leaves that are dipped in eau de vie, while **Cowgirl Creamery's St Pat** is encased in the leaves of nettles. Other cheeses like **Caprini Tartufo** are infused with the flavor of truffles. You could even argue

that **Vacherin Mont d'Or** (see page 18) is a flavored cheese because of the strip of spruce bark that is wrapped round the cheese before it is put in its box.

Another way to imbue flavor is to marinate small or cut cheeses in herb-flavored oil. You can buy these ready-made or make them yourself, as in the Marinated Feta with Herbs on page 141.

SMOKED CHEESES

Like other ingredients, cheeses can be smoked, a technique that tends to suit firmer cheeses, such as **Cheddar** or **Gouda-style** cheese, although you can buy smoked Mozzarella (**scamorza**) and smoked blues, a specialty of the Rogue Creamery in Oregon.

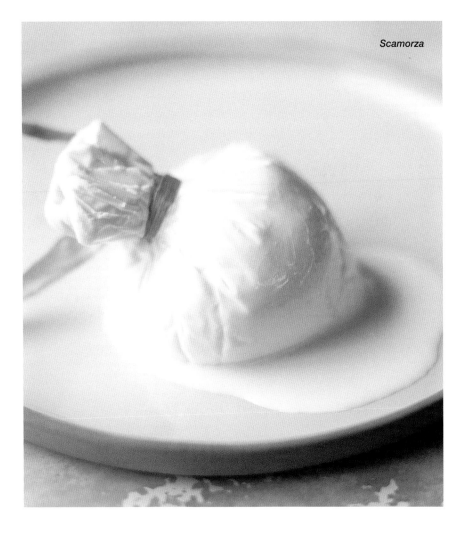

Scamorza

FIND YOUR TYPE OF CHEESE

Beaufort

Mature Gouda

As you will have seen from the preceding pages, there are many different styles of cheese and literally thousands of different cheeses—more than 1,000 in France alone! And given how different our taste buds are, it would be remarkable if we liked them all. Some people adore pungent, washed-rind cheeses, but to others their barnyardy smell is totally off-putting. Some love goat cheeses. Others hate them (although often that turns out to be because they've only tried a very mature "goaty" example).

Tastes evolve, so I would urge you to keep experimenting. If you think back to when you first tried coffee, you probably drank a mild, sweet, milky latte or cappuccino, then you might have dropped the sugar, reduced the milk, and ended up an espresso lover. The same thing can happen with cheese. Here are some first steps to take you out of your comfort zone.

IF YOU LIKE MILD CHEESE

You'll probably already like mild **goat cheeses**, mild **Cheddar**, **Camembert**, **Brie**, mild Swiss and Scandinavian cheeses, such as **Emmental** and **Jarlsberg**, and **Mozzarella**.
DO TRY: Young goat cheeses that are rolled in herbs or coated with ash. **Lancashire**, **Caerphilly**, and other British regional cheeses, **Beaufort** (a wonderful French Alpine cheese— one of my favorites), **Boursault** (a creamy French cow's cheese), and a mild **Taleggio** (a good substitute for Mozzarella on pizza). You might even put a toe in the water with one of the milder blues (see page 22).

IF YOU LIKE MELLOW CHEESE

You'll probably like a good **Cheddar**. **DO TRY:** Exploring Cheddars from different producers—it's fascinating how different they are. There are also cheeses you'd enjoy made in a similar style, like **Lincolnshire Poacher**. If you've dismissed **Gouda** as being too bland, try a mature one— it's a revelation, as is the award- winning **Uplands Pleasant Ridge** from Wisconsin.

Explorateur

Berkswell

Stinking Bishop

IF YOU LIKE GOOEY, INDULGENT CHEESE

You'll probably be a fan of mature **Brie** and **Camembert**.

DO TRY: Triple-crème cheeses, such as **Explorateur** and **Brillat-Savarin**. There's also a meltingly soft ewe's milk cheese called **Le Pérail** that you almost need to scoop up with a spoon. (**Torta del Casar** is another.) And you haven't lived until you've tried a **Vacherin Mont d'Or** (see page 18).

IF YOU LIKE SHARP CHEESE

You'll probably like **Feta** and **Pecorino** and may like salty blues, such as **Roquefort**.

DO TRY: Other hard sheep's and goat cheeses. You probably know about **Manchego** but try other Spanish cheeses, such as **Zamorano** and **Roncal**, along with **Berkswell** from England. You should also look out for a fabulous hard goat cheese called **Majorero** from the Canary Islands. And if you like **Roquefort**, you'll probably enjoy other sheep's milk blues, such as **Crozier Blue** from Ireland.

IF YOU LIKE STRONG CHEESE

You'll probably like all those smelly French cheeses, such as **Livarot**, **Munster**, and **Epoisses**.

DO TRY: Other washed-rind cheeses, such as **Stinking Bishop** from Gloucestershire and **Carré de l'Est**, an incredibly powerful (but delicious) beer-washed cheese from Northern France. (Wrap it up very well—even put it in a plastic box otherwise everyone will complain about the smell!) You should also look out for really well-aged hard cheeses, such as four-year-old **Parmesan**, **Roomano**, **Oude Gouda**, and **Vieux Mimolette**, and strong blues, such as **Cabrales** and **Valdeón**.

WHAT TO DRINK
WITH CHEESE

THIS PAGE *Sauternes with Roquefort*
LEFT *Irish whiskey with (clockwise from top)*
Cashel Blue, Ardrahan, and Gubbeen

MATCHING CHEESE AND WINE

If you asked your friends what food they most often associate with wine, I'm sure the majority would come up with cheese. But it's not always the perfect marriage it's held up to be. If you think for a moment about the average cheese board with five or six contrasting styles of cheese, it's a tall order to expect any one wine to match them all. And the better and more characterful the cheeses are, the harder it is—a dilemma for anyone who's both a cheese and a wine lover.

Even with the less challenging situation of a single wine and a single cheese, you can find that a match misfires. The wine has only got to be a shade past its peak or the cheese allowed to mature a few days longer than recommended for a promising relationship to break down before it's even off the starting blocks.

I tell you this not to discourage you—there are some truly wonderful cheese and wine matches out there—but to explain why the cheese course is so often a disappointment with your favorite wine.

The first thing to be aware of is that white wines often pair better with cheese than red ones do. This stands to reason if you think about the fruits that generally accompany cheese, for example apples, pears, grapes, and pineapple. Unoaked white wines in particular have a freshness and crispness that provide a perfect counterpoint to the rich, palate-coating texture of many cheeses.

Sweet wines too can work better with cheese than with a dry red, especially blues or other cheeses with a touch of bitterness that can clash horribly with the tannins in an oak-aged wine.

There are ways to encourage a red wine and cheese to match successfully and it's important to master them because your guests expect to enjoy the two together, but you need a bit of inside knowledge (see page 33).

A useful rule of thumb to help you make a successful match is that combinations of wine and cheese from the same region usually work. Good examples are **Gewurztraminer** and **Munster**, both from the Alsace region, **Chaource** and **Champagne**, **Crottin de Chavignol** and **Sancerre** from the Loire Valley, and a cheese fondue with a crisp dry **Savoie** or Swiss white. However, the Burgundian habit of serving **Epoisses** with fine local **red Burgundy** is not such a good idea. Personally, I think Epoisses is much better suited to **Marc de Bourgogne**, a grappalike spirit (see page 18).

Another strategy you can employ is to "build a bridge" between the cheese and the wine by introducing complementary ingredients that will facilitate the match. This, of course, has been done for years. The provision of bread (see page 67), crackers (see page 66), butter, and fruit, such as grapes and apples, all modify the taste of the cheese, but nowadays there are many more options in the form of fruit pastes and jellies which can bring even more wines into play. Take a look at the section on Entertaining with Cheese (pages 48–83) for some more ideas.

You can also make your wine and cheese matching easier by serving your cheeses in peak condition. I don't mean that they shouldn't be well matured, simply that they should be freshly bought and carefully stored. With a few exceptions such as Parmesan-style cheeses, cheese is best bought little and often (see page 149). Most cheese is also more wine-friendly if you remove the rind, although if that is an aspect you enjoy, simply choose a stronger drink to accompany it.

Essentially, it's less a question of following a set of "rules" than applying common sense. Milder cheeses are going to be much more accommodating with wine than stronger, more pungent ones. If you pair a **port** with a very young, moussey goat cheese, it will overwhelm it. If you eat a strong blue cheese with a light white wine, it will strip the wine of its flavor. Like all food and wine matching, it's a question of getting the balance right.

RIGHT *Red wine, Stilton, walnut bread, oat crackers, butter, walnuts, and damson paste*

RED WINE AND CHEESE

People want to drink red wine with cheese, full stop. It's such a long-held belief that the two go well together that it cannot easily be dislodged. But to avoid the almost inevitable disappointment that ensues, choose your cheeses and their accompaniments carefully.

There are three useful tips to bear in mind when choosing cheese to serve with red wine.

1. It's better to go for a hard rather than a soft or semisoft cheese.

2. Remember that it is easier to match red wine with cooked cheese dishes than with uncooked cheese, especially when the dish features red wine-friendly ingredients, such as beef or mushrooms.

3. It helps to introduce other elements on the plate that will assist the match. Breads of character, such as walnut or sourdough (especially toasted), good farmstead butter, and cooked fruits, such as pears in red wine and cherry compote, will all help kick your wine into touch, as will a few marinated black olives, if you like them.

Oh, and don't be afraid to serve a single cheese on its own (see the "hero" cheese board on page 55).

CHEESES THAT WORK BEST WITH RED WINE

◆ Hard sheep's cheese, e.g. Italian **Pecorino**, **Manchego**, and **Zamorano** from Spain, **Vermont Shepherd**, and British **Berkswell**: sheep's cheese is the most consistently successful match with red wine I've tried

◆ Well-aged cheeses that have a dry, crystalline texture, e.g. **Parmigiano-Reggiano**, aged **Gouda**, and **Mimolette** and **Sbrinz** from Italy,

Holland, France, and Switzerland respectively. Younger versions of these cheeses will also match quite well.

◆ Medium-matured cow's cheeses, such as milder **Cheddar** and **St George**

◆ Red wine-washed cheeses such as the Italian **Ubriaco** and Spanish **Murcia al Vino** (but not white wine-, brine-, beer-, or cider-washed ones)

◆ Mature or wrapped goat cheeses like **Banon**

◆ **Provolone piccante**

CHEESES TO AVOID WITH RED WINE

◆ Very oozy **Brie**- and **Camembert**-style cheeses

◆ Pungent washed-rind cheeses, such as **Epoisses** or **Langres**

◆ Strong blues, such as **Gorgonzola piccante** or **Roquefort**

RED WINES THAT WORK BEST WITH CHEESE

◆ Aged Tempranillo-based reds, such as **Rioja Reserva and Gran Reserva**

◆ Mid-weight Grenache-based reds, such as **Côtes du Rhône** and modern Spanish **Garnacha**

◆ Mourvèdre-based reds, such as **Bandol** (one of my own personal favorites with cheese)

◆ Slightly "porty" reds with rich brambly or figgy flavors, such as **Douro** reds, **Zinfandel** and **Amarone**, and southern Italian reds, such as **Aglianico** and **Negroamaro**

◆ There are circumstances in which other styles of red will work perfectly well with cheese too. Light, fruity reds, such as those from the Loire Valley and Beaujolais regions of France are good with goat cheese, for example.

◆ Inexpensive fruity reds, such as **Chilean Pinot Noir**, **Merlot**, and **Carmenère** can be enjoyable with a milder **Brie** or **Camembert**.

◆ A mature red **Bordeaux** can work well if none of the cheeses is too pungent. I recently successfully matched a six-year-old **Canon-Fronsac** with a cheese board of **Appleby's Cheshire**, **Waterloo** (a buttery semisoft cow's milk cheese), **Berkswell**, and **Cashel Blue**. The key was that the cheeses were all mellow and the wine had no harsh tannins.

◆ Even tannic young **Cabernet Sauvignon**, probably the most difficult red to pair with cheese, comes into its own with a steak or burger topped with melted blue cheese.

If you enjoy red wine and cheese but not always the two together, keep on experimenting! Look at the suggestions for berry-flavored drinks on page 41 for more inspiration.

LEFT *Red wine with Parmesan*

WHITE WINE AND CHEESE

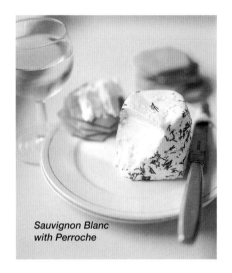

Sauvignon Blanc
with Perroche

Once you've tried white wine with cheese, you'll never look back. The first experience is likely to be a glass of Sauvignon Blanc with a goat cheese, an epiphany that should convert you at first sip. Once you've tried a crisp, fruity white with a fondue, or an Alsace Gewurztraminer with a pungent Munster you'll wonder why anyone drinks anything else.

The reason people are sceptical about accompanying cheese with white wine, as I've suggested on page 30, is that it seems slightly awkward to introduce a white wine at the end of a meal in which a full-bodied red has been served with the entrée. You don't want to switch back to a light, crisp white and I don't blame you. But there are many lighter meals with which you might be drinking white and carry on doing so through the cheese course, or simple snacks where all you need to do is pull a bottle of white wine from the fridge.

CHEESES THAT WORK BEST WITH WHITE WINE

◆ **Goat cheese** is the white wine cheese par excellence whether it's a few days old, a week old, or a month old (the latter can be interesting with older white wines). **Sauvignon Blanc** is the classic pairing but dry **Riesling** works well too.
◆ **Feta** and other white crumbly cheeses, such as **Caerphilly** and **Wensleydale**, also work well with crisp, fruity whites
◆ Alpine cheeses, such as **Gruyère**, **Comté**, and **Beaufort**, and French **tomme** and Italian **toma** cheeses all suit white wines better than red. Smooth, dry whites with good acidity work well here, as do slightly aromatic whites, such as Alsatian **Pinot Gris**.
◆ Mild to medium-matured **washed-rind cheeses** suit aromatic wines, such as **Pinot Gris** and **Gewurztraminer**. More pungent examples are better with Trappist beers (see page 42) or stronger drinks (see pages 39 and 45–46).

CHEESES TO AVOID WITH WHITE WINE

◆ **Blue cheeses** are not good with sharply flavored dry white wines. They don't do many favors to aged cheeses, such as **Parmigiano-Reggiano**, either.

WHITE WINES THAT WORK BEST WITH CHEESE

◆ Crisp, "neutral" dry whites with good acidity, such as **Pinot Grigio** and other dry Italian whites and the Spanish grape variety **Xarel-lo**, are good with salads or antipasti with cheese and mild crumbly white cheeses
◆ Dry whites from Switzerland and the Savoie region of France work well with **Alpine cheeses** and **cheese fondues**
◆ Fruity dry whites, such as **Sauvignon Blanc** and Greek **Assyrtiko**, are brilliant with **goat cheese** and Greek cheeses like **Feta** and **Halloumi**
◆ Aromatic off-dry whites, such as **Pinot Gris** and **Gewurztraminer**, pair well with washed-rind cheeses, such as **Munster**
◆ Dry **Rieslings** are a good alternative to Sauvignon Blanc with **goat cheese**
◆ Smooth dry whites, such as unoaked

Chardonnay and **Pinot Blanc** work well with egg dishes that contain cheese, such as omelet and quiche
◆ White **Bordeaux** can be a fine match for an old **Comté**, while a barrel-fermented **Chardonnay** is a surprisingly good match for a **full-flavored Cheddar** if you don't want to drink a port or a beer
◆ Southern French blends of **Roussanne, Marsanne,** and **Viognier** are a good alternative to reds with sheep's cheeses, such as **Manchego**

COOL NOT FREEZING COLD

We tend to think that all whites should be served well chilled but sometimes you can overdo it, particularly with more full-bodied or older whites whose opulent flavors can be dumbed down by being served too cold. While you can serve unoaked or aromatic whites like **Riesling** or **Sauvignon Blanc** at 46–50°F or after 2 hours in the fridge, fuller whites benefit from being served at 54–57°F or chilled for 1 hour 15 minutes –1 hour 30 minutes.

ROSE AND CHEESE

Now that rosé is so popular, it's more than likely you will find yourself drinking it with cheese but, like other types of wine, it won't go with everything. Light, dry rosés such as Provençal rosés will go with much the same sort of cheese—particularly **goat cheese**—as a fruity white would. A full-bodied, ultra-ripe **Cabernet** or **Syrah rosé** will behave more like a red, although you may find them more forgiving because of their fruitiness and absence of harsh tannins.

Cheeses that go well with rosé include those that you might pair with berry-flavored drinks (see page 41), particularly milder **Brie-** and **Camembert-style** cheeses, mild cheeses, such as **Chaource**, and creamy cheeses, such as **Finn** or **Explorateur**. Strong, dry rosés, such as those you find in Spain and southern France, are good with sheep's cheeses. Rosés are less successful with washed-rind and blue cheeses.

Rosé with a mild Camembert

SWEET WINE AND CHEESE

Why do sweet wines go so extraordinarily well with cheese? It's not just blues—although they are the outstanding match—but hard cheeses and washed-rinded cheeses too, as I discovered from a recent tasting I conducted: a superb Sauternes shone with almost every cheese we put with it, including a well matured Epoisses.

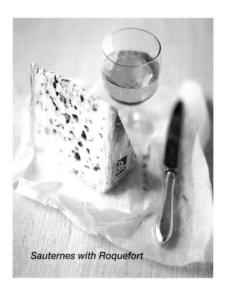

Sauternes with Roquefort

Certainly the lusciousness of many sweet wines helps to make them shine: it coats the palate with syrupy sweetness and diminishes the effect of any bitterness in the cheese. Many have fruit flavors that are naturally complementary to cheese, such as grapes, peach, apricot, and quince or, in the case of sweet red wines, plum and blackberries. And some have a crisp acidity that helps to counterbalance the semisoft texture of washed-rind cheeses that can so easily defeat a red.

I know there's still a residual feeling that sweet wines are not somehow serious, or a needless indulgence at the end of a long meal, but I would urge you to give them a try. I promise that your guests will be impressed!

CHEESES THAT WORK BEST WITH SWEET WINES

◆ Any blue cheese, whether it's crumbly like **Stilton** or **Fourme d'Ambert**, creamy like **Gorgonzola**, or salty like **Roquefort** will find a sweet wine partner
◆ Powerful washed-rind cheeses, such as **Epoisses** or **Munster**, work as well with a sweet wine as they do with an aromatic one like **Gewurztraminer**. Try them with a wine that's both sweet and aromatic, such as a **vendange tardive** (a late-harvest sweet wine) or a late-harvest **Gewurztraminer**, and the effect should be sensational!

◆ Sheep's cheeses can be highly enjoyable with sweet wine. Try an **Ossau-Iraty-Brebis** with a **Jurançon** or **Pacherenc du Vic-Bilh** from the south-west of France
◆ Aged **Parmigiano-Reggiano** and **Gouda** are delicious with a sweet red wine like **Banyuls** or **Maury**
◆ **Cheddar** is good with **port** but also works amazingly well with sweet wines like **Sauternes**

CHEESES TO AVOID WITH SWEET WINE

Nothing terrible happens but there are better things to drink with fresh young **goat cheeses** and delicately flavored cheeses, such as **Chaource.**

SWEET WINES THAT WORK BEST WITH CHEESE

◆ **Sauternes** and similar sweet wines from the Bordeaux region, like late-harvest **Sauvignon Blancs**. The classic pairing is **Roquefort** but, as I mentioned before, they go with a much wider range of blues—and other cheeses.
◆ Richly flavored sweet wines, such as **Tokaji** from Hungary, **Vin Santo**, and the exotic **Passito di Pantelleria** from the tiny island just off the Sicilian coast. Again, they are great partners for a **blue cheese** but a good companion for a carefully chosen cheese board or plate that includes strongly flavored cheeses.
◆ Sweet red wines, such as **Banyuls,**

Maury, and **Recioto** are interesting substitutes for port (see page 39) with **blue cheese** but they are also good with sheep's cheeses and aged cheeses, such as **Parmigiano-Reggiano** and **Mimolette**.
◆ Other sweet wines, such as southern French, Greek, and Spanish **Muscat**, will do a good job. You can also find some spectacular matches for aged **Riesling** although they do less well across the board. Matured **goat cheese**, **Alpine cheese**, and **hard sheep's cheese** work best.

ADD A LUSCIOUS FRUIT

A good tip when you are pairing food and wine is to introduce an ingredient that will create a link or "bridge" between the two, complementing the food and picking out flavors in the wine. With sweet wines and cheese, that could be a ripe peach or nectarine with a **Sauternes**, a few dried apricots (or nuts) with a **Tokaji**, or a cherry compote with a sweet red wine like **port** (see more suggestions on pages 51–67).

CHAMPAGNE AND CHEESE

It might surprise you to discover that Champagne can be excellent with cheese. I don't just mean with cheese canapés, such as gougères and crisp little cheese pastries whose "umami" (savory) flavors blend beautifully with the distinctive flavor of a mature sparkling wine. It also works well with a slightly chalky cheese, such as a **Chaource** (a classic match), a delicately flavored young goat cheese, or a double- or triple-crème cheese. If you're lucky enough to have a vintage Champagne on your hands, it will be sensational with an aged **Parmigiano-Reggiano** or a **Vacherin Mont d'Or**. For a Valentine's treat, try serving a truffle-infused cheese, such as a **Caprini Tartufo**, or a heart-shape **Cœur de Neufchâtel** with a **rosé Champagne**—a wonderful way to woo any cheese lover! (See also Cheese for Two on page 56.)

PORT, SHERRY, AND OTHER FORTIFIED WINES AND CHEESE

Port is so firmly associated with cheese that other fortified wines don't get a look-in, but sherry, Madeira, and similar wines can be just as successful. People can be a little reluctant to bring out a strong wine at the end of dinner, so I prefer to offer these pairings as an aperitif or an imaginative, between-meals snack—a late afternoon alternative to tea or even an indulgent midmorning offering for weekend guests if lunch is running late! A small glass of port or sherry and a nibble of cheese also make a nice nightcap if you've eaten early (but not too much of either or you may have a sleepless night!)

CHEESE TIP

You can enhance a match between cheese and a fortified wine by bringing in accompaniments that reflect the flavors in the wine: olives and almonds in the case of a fino sherry; raisins, dried figs, dates, or ready-to-eat prunes with stronger, sweeter sherries; a damson or cherry compote with a brambly, late-vintage port.

ABOVE *Malmsey Madeira with Roquefort, dried figs, and raisins*
LEFT *Fino sherry with Manchego, olives, and Marcona almonds*

CHEESES THAT WORK BEST WITH DRY, TANGY WINES (FINO AND MANZANILLA SHERRY AND SERCIAL MADEIRA)

◆ Hard Spanish and Basque sheep's cheeses, such as **Manchego** and **Ossau-Iraty** (especially with accompanying green olives and almonds)
◆ Aged goat cheeses
Less good with rich, creamy cheeses.

CHEESES THAT WORK BEST WITH DRY, NUTTY WINES (DRY AMONTILLADO, PALO CORTADO, AND DRY OLOROSO SHERRIES, VERDELHO MADEIRA AND 20-YEAR-OLD TAWNY PORT)

◆ Hard Swiss-style cheeses, such as cave-aged **Gruyère**, **Beaufort**, and **Comté**, **Cheddar**, **Red Leicester**
◆ **Gouda-style** cheeses, mature **Parmigiano-Reggiano**, and **Sbrinz**
Less good with young, moussey goat cheeses.

CHEESES THAT WORK BEST WITH PALE, SWEET WINES (CREAM SHERRIES AND WHITE PORT)

◆ Mild blues, such as **Gorgonzola dolce (Dolcelatte)**, **Cambozola**, and other **blue Brie**
◆ Mild, hard sheep's cheeses

Less good with mature **Cheddar** and strong blues.

CHEESES THAT WORK BEST WITH SWEET, NUTTY WINES (10-YEAR-OLD AND SOME 20-YEAR-OLD TAWNY PORTS)

◆ Mellow blues, such as **Stilton**
◆ Medium-matured **Cheddar** and **Gouda-style** cheeses, **Mimolette**
◆ Milder washed-rind cheeses
Less good with young goat cheeses, **Feta**, and other crumbly white cheeses.

CHEESES THAT WORK BEST WITH PLUM- AND BERRY-FLAVORED WINES (LATE-BOTTLED VINTAGE AND VINTAGE PORT)

◆ Blue cheeses, especially **Stilton**
◆ **Cheddar**
Less good with young goat cheeses but overall a pretty versatile all-rounder.

CHEESES THAT WORK BEST WITH SWEET, RAISINY WINES (SWEET OLOROSO AND PEDRO XIMENEZ SHERRIES, AND BUAL AND MALMSEY MADEIRAS)

◆ Tangy **Cheddar** and strong blues, such as **Roquefort** and **Cabrales**, especially with raisins, figs, or dates
Less good with young goat cheeses, **Brie**, **Camembert**, and garlic-flavored cheeses.

APPLE-FLAVORED DRINKS AND CHEESE

One of the best ways to grasp how cheese and drink pairing works is to focus on a single ingredient. Think about the various drinks that contain that flavor and how they might match with different cheeses.

A good example is apple, which turns up in a wide range of drinks. At one end of the spectrum you have fresh-tasting **apple juice**, which is well suited to daytime drinking and to young, fresh cheeses. At the other end you have an oak-aged drink, such as **Calvados** or **Applejack**, a full-strength liquor that

better suits after-dinner occasions and strong cheeses that can defeat red wines. In between these you have a range of apple-based drinks of different strengths—**hard cider**, **Pommeau**, or other apple-based aperitifs and **apple eaux de vie**, some of which can be turned into cocktails. You'll be surprised

APPLE JUICE

My own preference is for cloudy, **unfiltered artisanal apple juices**, which have a much truer, pure apple flavor. These are ideally suited to fresh young **goat or sheep's cheeses**, particularly in salads or light vegetable quiches. To dress up the apple juice, served it chilled in a pitcher with fresh apple slices, slices of lemon, and whole mint leaves.

CIDER

Ciders vary in style from mild mass-produced ciders to ultra-strong alcoholic hard ciders, taking in various degrees of sweetness in between. Let's pitch for a middle-of-the-road, **dry farmstead hard cider**, which is wonderful with a plate of **Cheddar** and apple chutney. Sparkling **Normandy cider** is a great terroir-based match for **Camembert**.

what successful matches can be made. For a drinks party with a difference why not arrange a cheese and apple evening, laying on different types of cheese and matching drinks? Or taste different hard ciders with different cheeses, served alongside a variety of apples from the farmers' market? It's great to be able to introduce your guests to new flavor combinations and it really gets people talking.

BERRY-FLAVORED DRINKS AND CHEESE

You could perform a similar exercise with berry-flavored drinks. Line up some **cranberry or pomegranate juice** (good with **cream cheese**), a **cherry or raspberry beer** (with **berry-topped cheesecake**), Pinot Noir (with a young Brie), and a **cherry liqueur** or a **vintage character or late-bottled vintage port** (with **blue cheese**).

CHEESE TIP

You need to think about the strength of both the drink and the cheese. A medium-matured Camembert, for example, would pair well with a medium hard cider, whereas a very well matured, unpasteurized one would pair better with a Pommeau or a Calvados.

APPLE APERITIFS

There is a wide range of apple-flavored aperitifs. Some, like **Pommeau**, are simply stronger versions of cider (or weaker versions of apple brandies if you like); others are more like an **apple-flavored eau de vie**. For a strikingly different drink, serve ice-cold shots of vivid **Apple Sourz** in martini glasses with crostini topped with **goat cheese** and diced apple.

APPLE BRANDIES

Apple brandies like **Calvados** and **Applejack** are particularly good companions for strong artisanal cheese, such as well-matured **Camembert fermier** or a powerful washed-rind cheese like **Pont-l'Evêque** (both from Normandy). Go for younger brandies rather than ones labelled "hors d'age" where the apple flavor is less evident.

BEER, CIDER, PERRY, AND CHEESE

It's hard for us wine lovers to accept, but beer and hard cider are every bit as good as wine with cheese, and in some cases even better. If you've ever tried a Camembert with hard cider or a "stinky" washed-rind cheese with a strong Belgian Trappist ale you'll know exactly what I mean. When I wrote my beer and food book *An Appetite for Ale* a couple of years ago, I was blown away by the combinations I discovered. The one problem is that there's still a bit of a stigma about bringing beer to the dining table but please don't be put off. With the increased interest in craft beers, I'm sure that will soon change.

British ale with Lincolnshire Poacher

CHEESES THAT WORK BEST WITH BEER

Some cheeses that cause problems with wine are outstanding with beer.
◆ Washed-rinded cheeses, such as **Epoisses** with strong, dark **Belgian Trappist beers** and French **Bières de Garde**. Some monasteries, like **Chimay**, produce both beer and cheese.
◆ Sharp **Cheddar** and similar cheeses, such as **Lincolnshire Poacher** and other full-flavored British territorial cheeses like **Lancashire**, pair well with traditional British ales
◆ Full-flavored blues, such as **Stilton** and **Blue Vinney**, are excellent with **barley wine** (see below), **porter**, and **Triple Bock**
◆ Mature **Gouda** and **Mimolette** are good with a strong, dark **Belgian beer** or a full-flavored **saison-style brew**

CHEESES TO AVOID WITH BEER

I wouldn't match fresh young goat cheeses with a robust porter or a strong blue with a lager.

BEERS THAT WORK BEST WITH CHEESE

◆ **Barley wine**, which is in fact a super-strong ale, is the port of the beer world. A great choice for a winter cheese board.
◆ **Porter** is a good all-rounder but pairs especially well with blues and rich, creamy cheeses like **Boursault**.
◆ **Oak-aged beer**, a relatively new category, works very well with sharp **Cheddar** and Cheddar-style cheeses
◆ **Amber ales and lagers**, also known as **bières ambrées**, work well with hard sheep's cheeses, such as **Ossau-Iraty** and **Berkswell**, and with **Gouda-style** cheeses. They're also a good partner for baked cheese dishes like lasagne.
◆ **Fruit beers**, especially raspberry and cherry—**Frambozen** and **Kriek**—pair with white-rinded cheeses, especially **Brie**, and with **goat cheese** salads
◆ Fresh, citrussy Belgian-style **witbier** (or **bières blanches** as they're also known) are fantastic with **goat cheese**
◆ You might think it would lead to a smoke overload but **smoked beer** works well with **smoked cheese**. It is also good with Alpine cheeses, such as **Gruyère** and **Comté**.

◆ **Chocolate and coffee beers** are stunning with **tiramisù**!

COOKING WITH BEER AND CHEESE

Beer is a good constituent of cheese recipes like Welsh Rarebit (see page 146), but also beer and cheese soups. Or you can make a fondue along the lines of the one on page 106.

CIDER, PERRY, AND CHEESE

Having a more limited range of flavors, **hard cider** and **perry** make less versatile companions to cheese than beer but where they do work, as with **Camembert** (see page 40), they work exceptionally well. Lacking the alcoholic strength of stronger ales, they are less successful with blues and pungent washed-rind cheeses.
◆ Enjoy **hard cider** with medium-sharp **Cheddar**, mild **Gouda-style** and Swiss cheeses, and hard sheep's cheeses (slices of apple will enhance the pairing)
◆ **Dry perries** pair particularly well with **goat cheese**

Hard cider with Camembert

WHISKEY AND CHEESE

Of all the foods that can show off a fine malt, cheese is by far the most congenial (to me, at least, although chocolate and whiskey lovers would probably want to argue their corner!) Of course, as with other liquors, there's the issue of introducing a new drink at the end of a meal, but as with fortified wine, I think it's an experience that works better on its own than as part of a meal. A couple of oatcakes or oat crackers (see page 136), smothered with Caboc or other creamy cheese, and a fragrant, floral malt or light, blended whiskey are a thoroughly appealing snack.

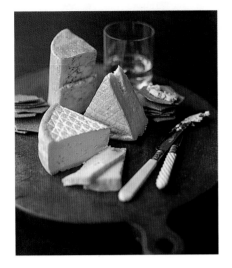

Irish cheese board: Irish whiskey with (clockwise from top) Cashel Blue, Ardrahan, and Gubbeen

If you want to make a real impact, you could create a terroir-based cheese board of Scottish cheeses with Scotch whiskey or Irish cheeses with an Irish one. For the Scottish board, I suggest **Lanark Blue**, an **Isle of Mull** or **Loch Arthur Cheddar**, and **Bishop Kennedy**, which is actually washed in whiskey. For the Irish board, see picture above: **Cashel Blue**, **Ardrahan**, and **Gubbeen** (oak-smoked if possible).

CHEESES THAT WORK WELL WITH WHISKEY

◆ Characterful blue cheeses, such as **Roquefort**, **Lanark Blue** (a great match with a peaty Islay whiskey like **Lagavulin**, see below), and mature **Stilton**
◆ Cream cheeses, from mild to double- or triple-crèmes like **Explorateur** work well with lighter, floral malts, as does the oatmeal-coated **Caboc**
◆ **Cheddar** is good with richer, fuller whiskies that are aged in sherry casks, like **The Macallan**
◆ **Smoked cheeses** work well with most whiskies other than intensely peaty ones

LEFT *Whiskey with Caboc and oatcakes*

CHEESES TO AVOID WITH WHISKEY

Steer away from more delicate cheeses that will be overwhelmed by the level of alcohol, for example young goat cheeses. And there are better drink partners for semisoft cheeses, such as **Vacherin Mont d'Or**.

WHISKIES THAT WORK WELL WITH CHEESE

◆ Lighter blends and floral whiskies, such as **Dalwhinnie** and **Glenkinchie** are the best styles to go for with creamy cheeses. Also good with **Parmigiano-Reggiano** and aged goat cheeses.
◆ Full, rich whiskies, whiskies aged in sherry casks, **Bourbon**: sharp **Cheddar** and **Gouda-style** cheeses, plus mellow blues, such as **Barkham Blue** and **Stilton**
◆ Peaty "island" whiskies: this is the style that really stands out with cheese, especially with strong blues, such as **Roquefort**, and salty cheeses, such as barrel-aged **Feta**. You can also try these whiskies with **Cheddar** and milder washed-rind cheeses.

DO YOU NEED TO DILUTE WHISKEY TO DRINK IT WITH CHEESE?

Purists would say "no" but it's a matter of taste. I like to reduce the alcohol of cask-strength whiskies, which can be up to 60 percent, and often add a splash of water to other malts to release their aromas and flavors. It's more common to dilute blended whiskies than malts but if you feel a whiskey is a little "hot," do add a splash.

OTHER OAK-AGED LIQUORS

Other oak-aged liquors are surprisingly good with cheese, especially **Calvados** and other apple brandies—the best match by far for a tricky-to-handle mature **Camembert** or its Normandy cousin, a mature **Pont-l'Evêque** (see page 41). Other brandies, such as **Cognac** and **Armagnac**, work well too, especially with washed-rind cheeses although I marginally prefer their less well-known counterpart, **Marc de Bourgogne**, an excellent match for an **Epoisses** or a **L'Ami du Chambertin**. You might also try a **Cheddar** or mature **Stilton** with a dark rum.

OTHER DRINKS THAT PAIR WELL WITH CHEESE

There are many other possible pairings with cheese. Here's just a taster.

FRUIT-FLAVORED EAUX DE VIE, SCHNAPPS, AND "BRANDIES"

Typically unoaked, the intense fruit flavors of **eaux de vie**, **schnapps**, and **aquavit** can work exceptionally well with cheese, my favorite pairing being **Pecorino** (or other sheep's cheese) and **Poire William**, the pear-flavored eau de vie from Alsace. Fruit "brandies" and flavored gins, such as **apricot brandy**, **cherry brandy**, and **sloe** and **damson gin**, tend to be less strong but equally appealing. Try **apricot brandy** with a full-cream cheese, such as **Boursault**, **cherry brandy** with **Brie** or hard sheep's cheese, and **sloe** or **damson gin** with **Stilton** (see opposite).

FRUIT WINES

Although made from fruits other than grapes, fruit or "country" wines can work in a very similar way to red table wine with the advantage that they lack the tannic structure that can make red wines such a problem with cheese. I particularly like **elderberry** and **blackberry wine** as an alternative to **port** with **blue cheese**, and **Japanese plum wine** (**umeshu**) with creamy **Brie**.

GRAPPAS AND UVE

Like **marcs** (see page 45), **grappas** are made from the skin, seeds, and stalks that are discarded from the wine-making process, but are less often oaked. **Uve**, like **eaux de vie**, are made from whole grapes. I particularly enjoy grappas and uve with Mediterranean

sheep's cheeses, such as the herb-coated **Fleur du Maquis** from Corsica.

GIN AND GENEVER

A surprising inclusion, you may feel, but the botanicals in **gin** and its Dutch counterpart, **genever**, play particularly well with strong washed-rind cheeses like **Epoisses** and **Munster** in much the same way as a **Gewurztraminer**. (My most exciting cheese pairing while writing this book was **Plymouth Gin** and a ferociously strong northern French cheese called **Carré de l'Est**.)

APERITIFS

Aperitifs are a particularly French and Mediterranean phenomenon that cover a wide range of drinks, from **Pommeau**, the rather attractive by-product of **Calvados** that goes similarly well with **Camembert** and washed-rind cheeses (see pages 40–41), to cherry-flavored **Guignolet** (delicious with **Brie**) and aniseed-flavored drinks like **pastis**, **ouzo**, and **raki** which tend to go well with salty sheep's cheeses, such as **Feta**, alongside other mezze. Off-dry **vermouths**, such as **Chambéry** and **Lillet Blanc**, are also pleasant with milder cheeses and cheese spreads.

SAKE

Another unlikely-sounding pairing but, thanks to its absence of tannins, **sake** fares much better than wine with many cheeses. One New York cheese shop, Murray's, holds regular sake and cheese

tastings. Try it with **Gruyère** and **Emmental**, with **tomme-style** cheeses, and with hard goat and sheep's cheeses, such as **Manchego**.

MEAD

Although there is a passionate following for mead (a beverage fermented from honey), it's hard to find specialist retailers. However, if you do come across a bottle, buy some and try it as a substitute for dessert wine with a mild to medium-strong **blue cheese**.

TEA

While not particularly to my taste, tea and cheese also has its advocates, especially the combination of strong, earthy **Pu'erh** with washed-rind cheeses. And if you're not a whiskey drinker but like the smokiness, try a cup of the equally pungent **Lapsang Souchong** tea rather than an Islay whiskey with **blue cheese**.

SOFT DRINKS

Almost all the flavors you find in wine you can find in soft drinks—and they will work with similar cheeses. A fragrant **elderflower cordial**, for example, is perfect with **goat cheese**; and **apple and pear juices** work with similar cheeses to hard cider. Meanwhile, **red grape**, **pomegranate**, **cranberry, and other berry-flavored juices** pair with just the same cheeses as light fruity reds, especially mild **Brie**.

ONE CHEESE, MANY POSSIBILITIES...

Just to show how there is no one single answer to a cheese pairing conundrum, here are 12 different possibilities with a single cheese. I've picked Stilton because it's a relatively easy cheese to match even though it's a blue, and you can take the pairing in a number of directions.

SWEET, BERRY-FLAVORED DRINKS

Port (vintage or late-bottled vintage)
The classic Stilton pairing—festive and warming. The velvety smoothness of a vintage port matches the rich creaminess of the cheese perfectly.

Elderberry wine
An old-fashioned drink but an underrated one that works better than most red table wines.

Sloe or damson gin
Lighter in alcohol than port but just as intensely flavored. One of my favorites and always brought out at Christmas.

RICH, RAISINY, AND NUTTY DRINKS

10- or 20-year-old tawny port
Having been aged in oak casks, these acquire a nuttier, more toffeeish flavor than ruby and vintage ports, which may appeal if you find those styles too sweet. Enhance the match with a selection of nuts and some figs or dates.

Sweet oloroso sherry or Madeira
With their sweet Christmas cake flavors, sweet oloroso sherries and Bual and Malmsey Madeira make just as enjoyable a partner for Stilton as port.

FRANGELICO

This sweet Italian hazelnut liqueur makes a way-out pairing for all you culinary thrillophiles out there.

SUMPTUOUS DESSERT WINES

Sauternes
With its luscious citrus and honey flavors, you might think Sauternes was too light to go with Stilton but it's a brilliant match.

Tokaji
Hungarian Tokaji has a different flavor profile—rich orange peel, dried apricot, and marmalade flavors. Another personal favorite.

Vin Santo
Italian wine and British cheese? The warm, rich flavors of Vin Santo make it a great combination. The more expected Italian blue, Gorgonzola, would work too.

FULL-FLAVORED, OAK-AGED LIQUORS

A rich sherry cask-matured malt
Whiskey is underrated as a partner for cheese. Many different styles would work with Stilton—including island whiskies—but this is the one I prefer.

Armagnac or Cognac
Each has its devotees but I'm a fan of the lesser-known and beguilingly varied Armagnac. Serve a few of the finest prunes, pruneaux d'Agen, on the side.

Demerara rum
Rarely paired with food but a fascinating partner for a mellow blue cheese, such as Stilton.

Pecorino, Sardinian carta da musica, and Vermentino

ENTERTAINING
WITH CHEESE

Brie, cherries, and Guignolet

A CLASSIC CHEESE BOARD

For any cheese lover, the idea of being able to work your way round a selection of contrasting cheeses is one of the best ways of indulging your passion. As a wine lover, I have some reservations about this but there are times when you just can't beat it.

The classic approach in putting together a cheese board is to aim for a contrast of textures, tastes, and shapes. Mild to strong, rounds and wedges, light against dark, soft and hard—it's about making an aesthetic impact as much as a gustatory one.

A classic cheese board will contain a cheese from one of each of the main styles. You can obviously leave out any you don't like or which you think will not go down well with your guests (washed-rind cheeses being the most likely candidates) but you should try to make sure there's something for everyone.

A CLASSIC SELECTION

Serve a young, fresh-tasting **goat cheese** (see page 14); a white or bloomy-rinded cheese, such as a **Brie** or a **Camembert** (see page 17); a hard cheese like a **Cheddar** (see page 21); and a blue, such as a **Stilton** (see page 22). You could also add a washed-rind cheese (see page 18); a sheep's cheese (see pages 14 and 21); or a cheese flavored with herbs (see page 25).

Traditionally, this choice might have been drawn predominantly from a country like France but there are now so many exciting new cheeses that there are many alternative countries from which to find them. You could include

cheeses from your own neighbourhood and from across the globe.

The picture opposite shows a classic board with something for everyone—from top left, a classic **Camembert**, **Tymsboro** (an ash-coated goat cheese from south-west England), **Colston Bassett Stilton**, **Montgomery's Cheddar** (also from south-west England), **Epoisses** (a washed-rind cheese from Burgundy), and **Sarriette de Banon** from Provence. The classic way to present them would be clockwise in order of flavor intensity (Tymsboro, Sarriette, Camembert, Cheddar, Epoisses, and Stilton) but I much prefer to arrange the board to show off the cheeses' different shapes, colors, and textures. You could, however, eat them in this order, sticking to the more easy-going cheeses (Tymsboro, Sarriette, Cheddar, and Stilton) if you were drinking red wine—see page 33 for why red wine can cause problems with cheese. Overall I think the best match for this particular selection would be a **vintage tawny port** or, you might be surprised to hear, a good **Sauternes** (see page 36). Remember the more mature a cheese is, the more difficult it can be to find a precise wine match so do consider other drinks (see page 46).

AN AMERICAN CHEESE BOARD

I suggest a fresh goat cheese like **Purple Haze** from Northern California, **Artisanal's Select American Camembert**, an **Uplands Pleasant**

Ridge alpine-style cheese from Wisconsin, **Cowgirl Creamery's Red Hawk** from California and a **Crater Lake Blue** from the Rogue Valley Creamery.

AN ITALIAN CHEESE BOARD

This might include a **Gorgonzola**, a semisoft **Taleggio**, **Pecorino Sardo** (hard sheep's cheese), and a **Caprini Tartufo** (truffle-infused goat cheese).

AN ANIMAL-LED CHEESE BOARD

While it is traditional to mix cheeses from different animals—goat, cow, and sheep—it's possible with the multitude of new cheeses that are being produced to base a board purely on sheep's or goat cheeses, or a mixture of the two— a boon to those who find themselves intolerant to cow's milk (see page 152).

A North American example might be **Humboldt Fog** goat cheese from Cypress Grove, a **Nancy's Hudson Valley Camembert** (sheep), **Elk Mountain Gruyère-style goat cheese**, Haystack Mountain's bloomy-rinded goat cheese **Haystack Peak**, and a **Vermont Shepherd** from Major Farms.

A SURPRISE SELECTION

As you become more knowledgeable about cheese, it's fun to mix the familiar and the unfamiliar. Try serving a new discovery from the farmers' market or a rare **Spanish or Portuguese cheese** alongside an old favorite that you know everyone loves.

LEFT *(Clockwise from top left)* Camembert, Tymsboro, Colston Bassett Stilton, Montgomery's Cheddar, Epoisses, Sarriette de Banon

CONTEMPORARY CHEESE BOARDS

Even ardent cheese lovers tend to be quite conservative about the way they serve cheese, sticking to the classic formula of having several different types of cheese from different countries and serving them on wooden boards (see page 51). But over the past few years I've come across many new and different ways of presenting cheese. Restaurants nowadays are much more imaginative about the surfaces they use, the way they cut cheeses, and the accompaniments they put with them, and these innovative ideas can suggest new and exciting ways to serve cheese at home.

At Alain Ducasse's eponymous restaurant at The Dorchester in London, for example, I was served a "tray" of four different cheeses with accompanying relishes: **Valençay** goat cheese with sweet pepper relish; **Montgomery's Cheddar** with poached grapes and Muscat wine jelly; a three-year-old **Vieux Comté** with a paste made from hazelnuts and vin jaune (a matured, sherrylike French white wine); and **Stilton** with Mostarda di Cremona (preserved fruit infused with mustard oil, typically from Cremona in northern Italy).

At the Auberge du Paradis, an innovative French restaurant in Saint-Amour-Bellevue in the Beaujolais region of France, the cheeses—**Valençay**, **Brillat-Savarin**, and **Vacherin Mont d'Or** with a dusting of paprika—arrived on a slate board with a spoonful of mirabelle (plum) purée and a cumin seed-crusted breadstick.

You don't have to attempt such fancy presentation but you can gain inspiration from them and adapt them to create a cheese board that will be a real talking point for your guests. Here are some ways to do it.

DIFFERENT SURFACES

There's no reason why a cheese board, which is merely shorthand for a selection of cheeses, should actually be a wooden board. It could be a tray, a basket, a series of tiles, glass, or a slate.

Slate is my own personal favorite. It's sophisticated and elegant and looks wonderful against the whites and grayish blues of goat cheeses, white-rinded cheese, and blues. Think in terms of ash-covered pyramids, such as **Valençay**, a bloomy-rinded cheese like **Waterloo**, **Morbier** with its distinctive streak of ash running through the middle, and the Vermont blue, **Bayley Hazen Blue**. Add a contrasting selection of pale celery and charcoal crackers and maybe a violet-colored velvety fresh fig or two and you've got a strikingly beautiful presentation.

DIFFERENT SHAPES

I'm thinking less of the shapes of the cheeses themselves here but the way you cut or scoop them (a spoon is an underrated implement when it comes to dealing with gooey cheeses like the runny sheep's milk **Le Pérail**!)

Hard cheeses, such as **Parmigiano-Reggiano**, can be shaved with a cheese slicer or a specially designed Parmesan knife; washed-rind cheeses can be cut into fine slices (though don't do this too far in advance of bringing it to the table or it will dry out). For more ideas on cutting and displaying cheese, see page 151.

Don't be afraid to upturn cheeses either. Wedges look dramatic propped on their base, point upwards: take a look at the presentation on the websites of some of the more innovative cheese retailers, such as The Fine Cheese Company, Neal's Yard Dairy, and New York's Artisanal (see Cheese Suppliers and Websites on page 158).

FEWER CHEESES

Smaller selections have significant advantages. They're cheaper, obviously, you're more conscious of the flavors of each individual cheese but, lastly and most importantly, you can design them to accompany a particular style of wine.

It's a strategy that I think works particularly well with red wine, which tends to clash horribly with certain cheeses (see page 33) or with awkward customers such as washed-rind cheeses or strong blues.

If you wanted to carry on drinking the fine red you had served with the entrée,

RIGHT *(Clockwise from top right) Morbier, Waterloo, Barkham Blue, and Tymsboro with charcoal crackers and fresh figs*

Cheese and sherry flight, from left: Oude Gouda and dry oloroso, Gorgonzola and cream sherry, Manchego and fino

you could serve a firm-slicing **goat cheese**, a **Pecorino**, and a piece of aged **Gouda**, for instance. Alternatively, if you had a delicious sweet wine, you might want to lay on a selection of three contrasting blues (see page 36).

And there's no reason why your accompaniment shouldn't be a beer. Pick three contrasting hard cheeses, say a **Comté**, a **Gouda-style cheese**, and a **Cheddar** and serve them with a **barley wine** or a strong **Belgian Trappist beer** (see page 42).

WINE AND CHEESE "FLIGHTS"

A brilliant idea for wine and cheese lovers pioneered by the innovative Artisanal cheese shop and bistro in New York, is to arrange a wine and cheese "flight." This is a selection of three different wines and cheeses served in small quantities to taste and compare. Usually the wines will be of a similar type, for example three or four wines made from the same grape—say Syrah or Shiraz—or four wines of different types from the same wine region, say the Loire. You can look at Artisanal's current suggestions on their website (www.artisanalbistro.com) or invent your own.

The idea applies equally well to other drinks. Why not try a sherry and cheese flight using some of the suggested pairings on page 39, a whiskey and cheese flight (see page 45), or an apple-flavored drinks and cheese flight (see pages 40–41).

FOLLOW THE SEASONS—AND THE WEATHER

Cheese, as I've already pointed out on pages 12–13, is seasonal, but perhaps even more importantly, from the point of view of the cheese lover, it needs

to adapt to the weather. Just as with other foods, one is drawn to different cheeses depending on whether it's cold or hot and sunny. (In general, these temperatures coincide with winter and summer but the climate is so variable nowadays that you could find yourself basking in the fall or freezing in the early spring!)

I tend to prefer lighter, younger, fresher-tasting cheeses like goat and sheep's cheeses when it's hot; and stronger, more mature cheeses, such as washed-rind cheeses, aged hard cheeses, and blues when the temperature drops below freezing (and Swiss cheeses but that's a question of mood as much as taste).

For a warm-weather cheese board you could offer a goat cheese, a hard sheep's cheese, and a jar of Marinated Feta with Herbs (see page 141) with a glass of rosé; on a chilly night you could serve an **Appenzeller**, a **Taleggio**, and a **Gorgonzola**—perhaps with a warming glass of **grappa** or **schnapps**! See also the suggestions for seasonal cheese plates on pages 60–61 and for Festive Cheese on page 83.

A LOCAL CHEESE BOARD

I've already suggested basing a cheese board on a specific country (see page 51), as it's easy enough to find five or six contrasting cheeses. But if you want to serve entirely local cheeses—and that's a nice thing to do—it's better to think of serving two or three, preferably with a locally produced drink (beer or fruit wines may be easier in some areas than wine), a locally made chutney or relish, and some locally baked (or homebaked) bread. If you have a particularly good local cheese maker, you could base your cheese board on their cheeses.

AN ADVENTUROUS CHEESE BOARD

This is one for friends who are really into cheese. Try to find some obscure cheeses they'll never have heard of or source them from a country whose cheeses are less well known—like Canada, Sweden, Spain and Portugal. Cheeses I've tasted recently that fall into this category include **Tiger Blue** from British Columbia, **Svecia** from Sweden, **Ilha Graciosa** from the Azores, and **Afuega'l pitu** from the Asturias region of Spain. That should impress any cheese connoisseur!

A "HERO" CHEESE BOARD

If you have found an exceptional cheese, there's an argument for making it the only one on the board so that your guests really have the opportunity to appreciate it without the flavor of other cheeses getting in the way. It also makes it more likely that you will finish it and avoid wasting what may be an expensive buy.

Against that you could argue that there may well be people present who might not like that type of cheese or who may not be able to tolerate it for dietary reasons (see page 152) so you probably have to know your guests well to do this. I wouldn't be inclined to offer a very strong blue, for example, as my only cheese (although a Stilton at Christmas is traditional), nor a pungent washed-rind cheese.

Good cheeses to feature in a solo role are a well-matured (but not over-runny) **Brie de Meaux** or **Camembert**, a fine **St George**, a visually striking cheese, such as **Mimolette** or **Morbier** with its distinctive line of ash running across its middle, or an aged **Parmigiano-Reggiano**, a choice that will flatter a fine red wine. A **Vacherin Mont d'Or** also deserves to stand on its own.

CHEESE FOR TWO

We tend to think in terms of large numbers for cheese boards but it's surprising how often you serve it just for two. Cheese is an indulgent treat which will make any cheese lover feel pampered and is an easy-to-prepare part of a romantic dinner.

One's instinct when catering for just two people is simply to buy less cheese but while that can be a good strategy with the right cheese (see the "hero" cheese board on the previous page), if you're entertaining, particularly if it's a romantic occasion, it could seem ungenerous.

What I like to do is create a miniature cheese board, which could be on a small butcher's block or a slate. Rather than putting out big pieces of cheese, I usually cut them into one-portion wedges or slices and put two of each on the board.

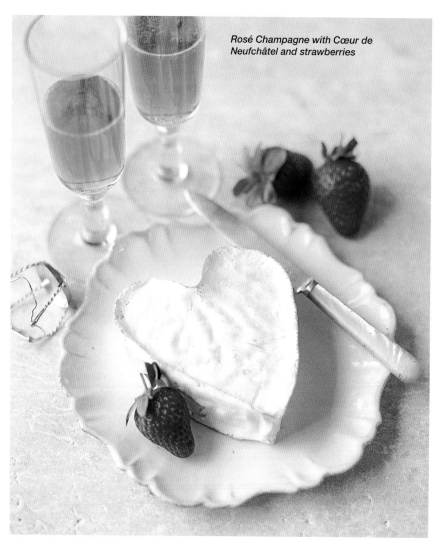

Rosé Champagne with Cœur de Neufchâtel and strawberries

A GENEROUS CHEESE BOARD FOR TWO

You could have two **goat cheese buttons**, two wedges of **Camembert** or other white-rinded cheese, two slices of **Beaufort**, and two radicchio leaves topped with a spoonful of a soft blue cheese, such as **Gorgonzola** or **Cashel Blue**. Perch two pots of fruit compote or chutney alongside, or a couple of Grape Jellies (see page 145), add a few grapes or a couple of fresh figs, some small homebaked rolls or pre-cut slices of raisin bread, and some rustic artisanal breadsticks and you've got a very pretty-looking board indeed.

A ROMANTIC CHEESE PLATE FOR TWO

For a more romantic occasion, you could serve the heart-shape **Cœur de Neufchâtel** or a truffle-infused cheese, such as **Caprini Tartufo**. Alternatively, slice a small, deep, round cow's cheese into horizontal slices and sandwich with fine shavings of black truffles, press together, wrap in plastic wrap, and refrigerate overnight for the flavor of the truffles to infuse the cheese. Serve with **rosé Champagne**.

A SUMMER CHEESE BOARD FOR TWO

For a summer date, think of partnering cheese and berries: indulge your partner with fine wedges of **Chaource**, wild strawberries, and a glass of **pink fizz** or treat him or her to a romantic breakfast of Raspberry and Ricotta Hotcakes (see page 128).

A MINI-FONDUE FOR TWO

Sometimes the simplest ideas are the most delicious! You can bake a whole **Camembert** and it will taste like the most fabulous fondue. Simply take the cheese out of its box and remove the wrapping. Replace the cheese in the box and lightly rub the surface with a cut clove of garlic, pierce the surface of the cheese with a skewer in a few places, then put the lid of the box back on. Bake it in a preheated oven at 400°F for about 25 minutes until the cheese is gorgeously gooey. Serve with crusty bread and breadsticks or tiny boiled new potatoes to dip into the hot, molten filling.

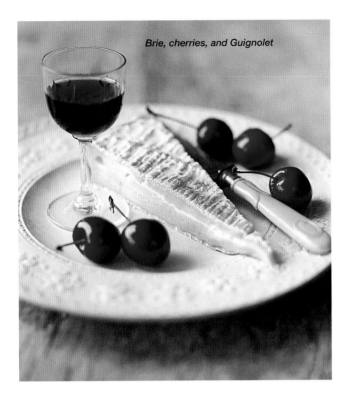

Brie, cherries, and Guignolet

CHEESE PLATES

The difference between a cheese plate and a cheese board is not the surface on which it's presented but the fact that each person's cheese is served individually rather than put out in the middle of the table to share. In my view it's a better way of handling the cheese course, particularly in the middle of a dinner party. You don't have to buy as much cheese, you can create a perfect balance of ingredients on the plate, it works better with wine or other drinks, and it looks great too.

A cheese plate is also a stylish way to enjoy a small snack of cheese. A hunk of cheese cut from the fridge and an apple may satisfy the hunger but if you're offering it to guests you want to make it look a bit more elegant.

You can borrow any of the ideas from elsewhere in the book—for example the Contemporary Cheese Boards on page 52, the Seasonal Cheese Salads on pages 94–95, or the country-based suggestions on page 51—and scale them down for a cheese plate, but one of the best ways of creating interesting combinations of flavors is to look to the season for inspiration (see overleaf).

You can also create a plate to match a particular type of wine or other drink. You'll find many suggestions in the What to Drink with Cheese chapter on pages 28–47.

LEFT Poire William with Pecorino and pears

DISCOVERING NEW COMBINATIONS

The best way to discover great pairings is to experiment. If you find a delicious new cheese, try different drinks with it. If you buy a beautiful bread or some unusual crackers, ask the store what cheese they would recommend with them. If you bring home a new wine, pour half a glass and try it out with any cheeses you have in the refrigerator. Here are some unusual combinations I've discovered in this way.

◆ **Morbier** is kinder to **red wine** than many washed-rind cheeses
◆ Smoked oatcakes make a great base for a creamy cheese, topped with a curl of wafer-thin smoked salmon, and accompanied by a mild **whiskey**
◆ **Gin**, of all drinks, is a good counterfoil to a pungent **washed-rind cheese**
◆ **Elderflower** is as sympathetic to **goat cheese** as **Sauvignon Blanc**

IN THE SPRING

Spring is the time we all want to enjoy the first of the new season's produce, which happily pairs perfectly with the new young cheeses. Decorate your cheese plates with leaves and herbs, accompany them with crisp, fresh white wines, and celebrate the end of winter.

◆ Serve a broiled slice of **goat cheese** marinated in oil with a herb salad or steamed or charred asparagus. Alternatively, scatter fresh goat cheese or a **white crumbly cheese** over a few mixed salad leaves. Perfect with **Sauvignon Blanc** or an aromatic **Belgian wheat beer**.

◆ Serve two contrasting **goat cheeses** for comparison—one very young and still soft, the other firmer and more mature with rosemary-flavored crackers and some herb-marinated olives. Try a crisp **rosé** this time.

◆ Do as the Italians do and serve cooked, peeled fava beans, fine slices of **Pecorino**, and shards of Sardinian *carta da musica* with a glass of **Vermentino** *(pictured above)*

◆ Another simple but sophisticated Italian idea for an aperitivo: strips of focaccia, **Parmesan** shavings, and a glass of **Prosecco**

IN THE SUMMER

Take advantage of the wealth of fresh fruit and vegetables to show off your cheeses: fresh berries, watermelon, peaches, apricots, tomatoes, and bell peppers. Don't be afraid to introduce a touch of spice. Chile and garlic work with cheese.

◆ Serve thinly sliced **sheep's cheese** with broiled bell peppers and almonds as a mini tapas plate with a glass of **fino sherry**. Or do as the Basques do and serve it with a cherry compote and a glass of **fruity red wine**.

◆ Serve British "ploughman's" platters with a good chunk of **Cheddar**, thickly carved ham, a spoonful of chutney, an apple, some crusty bread, and traditional **English ale**

◆ Serve a mini antipasto plate with slices of fennel, salami, **mozzarella**, and broiled artichokes or slow-roasted tomatoes and breadsticks. Drink a **light Italian red or white** with this.

◆ Plate up wedges of watermelon, crumbled **Feta**, pumpkin seeds, olive oil, and balsamic vinegar *(pictured above)*

◆ Serve a creamy cheese, such as **Explorateur**, **Robiola**, or **Brillat-Savarin** with a peach and a glass of **dessert wine**

◆ A show-stopper: a wedge of **Brie**, some fresh cherries, and a small glass of **Guignolet** or a **Belgian cherry beer**

IN THE FALL

Fall is the prime time for some of the ingredients that go best with cheese: apples, pears, grapes, figs, and nuts.

◆ Serve a wedge of ripe **Camembert** with sautéed apple slices and a glass of **Pommeau**

◆ A classic but none the worse for it: thin slices of **Manchego** with membrillo (quince paste) and a **palo cortado sherry**

◆ Try ripe pears, **Pecorino**, and chilled **Poire William**: clean and simple

◆ Fresh or broiled figs with **Gorgonzola** and a glass of **Maury**, a sweet red wine from the Roussillon region of France *(pictured above)*

◆ Give your cheese an Indian twist: try a washed-rind cheese like **Munster** scattered with roasted cumin seeds, served with mango chutney, and strips of warm naan bread. Serve with **Gewurztraminer** or a hoppy **Indian pale ale**.

◆ Two different **blues**—one cow's milk, one sheep's milk— with a mixed leaf and walnut salad drizzled with a walnut oil dressing. Surprisingly good with a full-bodied **Chardonnay**.

◆ A cheese and jelly plate: Grape Jellies (see page 145) and **Brie**. Sauternes jelly and **Stilton**.

IN THE WINTER

Winter cheese plates can take advantage of all the preserved fruits that are available—luscious big raisins, dates, and figs —as well as an array of fortified wines and liqueurs that come out at this time of year (see also Festive Cheese on page 83).

◆ A Spanish trio of **Cabrales** (one of the world's best blues), raisins, and **Pedro Ximénez sherry**

◆ A striking combination: **Fourme d'Ambert**, toasted walnut bread, poached kumquats, and **Grand Marnier**

◆ **Stilton**, oatmeal crackers, and **sloe or damson gin**—a great combination and just as good as port

◆ **Stilton** and **barley wine** (a strong ale). Strong ales are wonderful with blue cheese.

◆ Two stylish Italian ways of serving **Gorgonzola**. Drizzle with chestnut honey and serve with griddled panettone and **Vin Santo**, or serve with a thin wedge of panforte and a glass of **Marsala**.

◆ Fine slices of **Mimolette** or **Oude Gouda** with Medjool dates, dried figs, nuts, and **tawny port** *(pictured above)*

◆ A nibble of good farmstead **Cheddar**, Brazil nuts, and sweet **oloroso sherry**

Summer berries with ricotta and honey

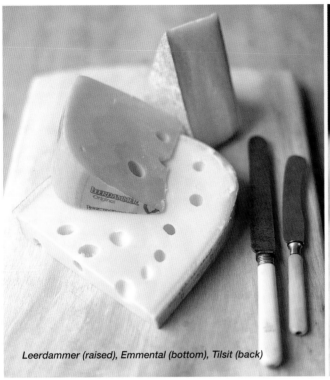

Leerdammer (raised), Emmental (bottom), Tilsit (back)

Prosecco with different types of cheese bagel

BREAKFAST AND BRUNCH

If you're not used to it, the idea of starting the day with cold meats and cheeses may seem strange but in many countries such as Holland, Germany, and Scandinavia it's quite traditional. It's certainly a sustaining way to "break your fast" and much easier than the traditional cooked breakfast to prepare for a crowd.

Mild, sliceable cheeses, such as **Tilsit**, **Emmental**, and **Leerdammer** work better at this time of day than stronger washed-rind cheeses or blues, which provide the palate with rather too emphatic a wake-up call! Light, mild, soft cheeses, such as **ricotta** and **fromage frais**, are also good at breakfast time, especially with fruit. A big bowl of lowfat fromage frais and another of mixed strawberries, raspberries, and blueberries makes a lovely centerpiece for a summer breakfast table or brunch. Alternatively, an idea I picked up from The Old Convent hotel in Ireland is to make fresh fruit "martinis" by spooning fromage frais into martini glasses and topping up with a selection of freshly cut fruit.

Treat weekend guests to a batch of the delicious Raspberry and Ricotta Hotcakes on page 128. They're equally good made with frozen raspberries and can provide a welcome reminder of summer on a dreary, cold, gray morning. Or serve a winter dried fruit compote with spoonfuls of mascarpone mixed with milk to make a spoonable consistency, and flavored with a dash of vanilla extract and a little sugar or honey.

And if you do want to serve more of a entrée, there's nothing nicer—or simpler —to make than a fluffy cheese omelet. Try the Goat Cheese Omelet with Wild Garlic and Chervil or some Buckwheat Galettes with Prosciutto and Emmental (both on page 101).

For a variety of brunch bagels, see the following page (and the picture above).

SANDWICHES AND SNACKS

You don't really need me to tell you how to make a cheese sandwich but there may be variations on the theme that might not have crossed your mind.

First, it's worth tailoring your bread to your cheese (see page 67). In general, softer and sliced breads are better with harder cheeses, and crustier breads like baguettes and ciabatta with soft or semisoft cheeses. (The more moist the filling, the drier the bread you need.)

A SORT OF PAN-BAGNAT

Pan-bagnat is traditionally a loaf of bread stuffed with Niçoise-style salad, but the options are endless. Many stores now sell big, flat rustic loaves that you can slice horizontally and fill with broiled or roast vegetables, such as zucchini, eggplant, onions, and bell peppers, scatter with basil leaves, and top with slices of **Mozzarella**. Press down firmly, wrap tightly in foil, and refrigerate for an hour, then cut into wedges or slices.

CLASSIC HERO SANDWICH

This is a great vehicle for cheese. Fill a sub or torpedo roll with slices of salami, ham, and/or mortadella, then top with slices of mild Swiss cheese like **Emmental** and finely sliced sweet pickles. Another deli-inspired classic would be to fill a freshly baked ciabatta with chargrilled steak and onions topped with melted **blue cheese**.

SALAD ROLLS

Any combination of ingredients that makes a good salad tends to taste pretty good wedged between two slices of bread or in a roll. **Mozzarella**, tomatoes, and basil, for instance,

(try making this with slow-roasted tomatoes for a change) or a chicken Caesar sandwich—sliced chicken breast, shaved **Parmesan**, shredded lettuce, and Caesar dressing.

CLASSIC SANDWICH FILLINGS

Other good, simple fillings include **Cheddar** with homemade apple or tomato chutney (great with white sliced bread); **blue cheese** with celery; and **cream cheese** with watercress (both the latter are good with brown bread); and a long slice of baguette with **Brie** and a spoonful of cranberry sauce makes an excellent snack over Christmas. For toasted sandwiches, such as paninis, see page 69.

A CHEESE AND BAGEL BRUNCH

Try this great—and easy to execute—idea for brunch (see picture on page 63). Serve three kinds of bagels: the traditional smoked salmon, **cream cheese** (mixed with finely chopped onion), and slices of sweet and sour cucumber; a whole-wheat bagel filled with a mild, creamy blue cheese, such as **Dolcelatte**, fine slices of air-dried ham and sliced fresh figs; and cinnamon bagels filled with **cream cheese** mixed with chopped, candied pecans or walnuts and fresh Medjool dates. (If you can't find candied nuts, warm pecans or walnuts in a skillet with a little sugar and shake until the sugar has dissolved and coated the nuts.) Offer **Prosecco** or other sparkling wine, fresh orange juice, and coffee.

CHEESE TIP

If you base your sandwich on more conventional fillings, such as ham and Swiss cheese, or smoked salmon and cream cheese, try putting it in a less conventional bread like a croissant or a bagel. For more bread suggestions, see page 67.

RIGHT *A pan-bagnat-style sandwich with zucchini, eggplant, onions, bell peppers, fresh basil, and Mozzarella*

CRACKERS AND CHEESE

Choosing a specific cracker to go with your cheese, an idea pioneered by the innovative The Fine Cheese Co. in Bath, south-west England, has really taken off in recent years and can turn a simple snack into a gourmet offering. Here are some combinations that work well.

◆ **Charcoal crackers** with young **goat and sheep's cheeses** (it's the visual contrast of black against white as well as the taste that's so appealing)

◆ **Celery crackers** with **Stilton** and other creamy blue cheeses

◆ **Fennel-, caraway- or cumin-spiced crackers** with washed-rind cheese

ABOVE *(From left) flatbread and goat cheese, sweet whole-wheat crackers and Cheddar, charcoal crackers and Perroche, baguette and Brie, walnut and raisin bread and Stilton, ciabatta and Mozzarella*

◆ **Chive crackers** with **Brie**

◆ **Oatcakes** with rich, creamy cheeses (and smoked oatcakes with blue cheese and crispy bacon!)

◆ **Sweet whole-wheat crackers** and **Dry Monterey Jack**

◆ **Scandinavian-style crispbreads** with mild semisoft cheeses like **Havarti**

◆ **Seeded, crisp flatbreads** with creamy **cow's, goat, or sheep's cheeses**

◆ **Breadsticks** and **Mozzarella**

When you're choosing a cracker, think about the texture as well as the flavor. Softer, spreadable cheeses need a firm base that won't crumble, while harder cheeses can be on a slightly more crumbly cracker like an oatcake or a savory whole-wheat cookie. It's also impressive—and easy—to make your own, which you can do well in advance (see page 136).

BREAD AND CHEESE

Isn't this the best ever combination—a simple pairing of artisanal ingredients that makes a perfect meal without the slightest effort? But there are so many cheeses—and so many breads. The most flexible type of bread in my view is a rustic country loaf, which could be an unbleached white, a mixture of flours, or a sourdough. As a general rule, crusty bread like baguette works better with softer cheeses, while firmer breads seem a better complement to harder cheeses.

◆ **Baguette** with **Brie** and **Camembert**

◆ **Traditional white loaves** are the traditional choice for **Cheddar, Double or Single Gloucester**, and other **hard cow's milk cheeses**.

◆ **Sourdough bread** goes with all kinds of cheeses, particularly **washed-rind** and **hard sheep's cheeses**

◆ **Walnut bread or walnut and raisin breads** are flexible but particularly good with **blue cheeses** and **goat cheeses**

◆ **Mixed grain breads** suit hard cheeses, such as **Cheddar, St George**, and **Pleasant Ridge Reserve**

◆ **Rye bread**—light rye goes with Alpine cheeses like **Beaufort** and **Comté**; dark rye with creamy, spreadable cheeses

◆ **Rye breads with caraway or fennel seeds** (see page 132) work with **washed-rind** and **sheep's cheeses**

◆ **Spiced sweet breads** e.g. *pain d'épice* complement **Roquefort** and other strongly flavored blues

◆ **Dense fruit breads** pair well with creamy blues, such as **Stilton**

◆ **Soft or crisp flatbreads and breadsticks** go with **soft goat cheeses** and **labneh** (see page 140)

◆ **Olive or rosemary-flavored breads** suit tangy sheep's cheeses like **Feta**

◆ **Ciabatta** and **Mozzarella** are made for each other

Introduce some variety into your bread basket by adding slices of toast.

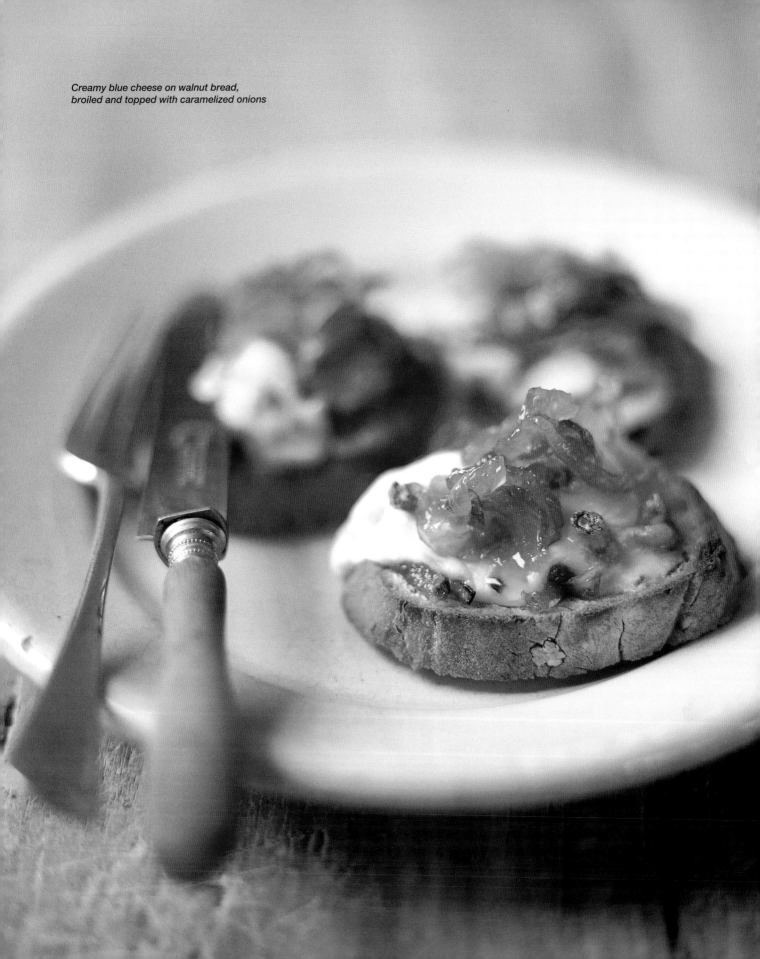

*Creamy blue cheese on walnut bread,
broiled and topped with caramelized onions*

CHEESE ON TOAST

Some form of cheese and toasted bread is probably in all our culinary repertoires, whether it's a simple case of laying slices of cheese on a piece of toast and popping it under the broiler or making a "toastie" or a panini in an electric sandwich toaster or contact grill. Often it's a question of finding a use for some leftover cheese and less than fresh bread, but it can be a great deal more than that.

If you're making cheese on toast for guests, try using a strong rather than a mild cheese for a change. Washed-rind cheeses, such as **Maroilles** and **Taleggio** melt beautifully over a piece of toasted sourdough bread, for instance. (You can even rub a little raw garlic on the surface of the bread if you're a garlic fan!) Creamy blue cheeses are great broiled or melted on toasted walnut bread—a good way of using up the remnants from a cheese board. You could add a layer of caramelized onions on top of the melted cheese to make a more substantial snack or appetizer.

Try introducing other ingredients to your toasted sandwiches too to make them more interesting. Crispy bacon, fried apple slices, and an Alpine cheese, such as **Beaufort**, for example, are delicious in a toasted ciabatta or panini roll, as are broiled vegetables with **Mozzarella** and broiled portobello mushrooms with **Taleggio**. (Almost anything you can put into a pizza you can put into a panini.)

SOUP, CROSTINI, AND CROUTONS

It's also useful to have a supply of crostini and croutons on hand to serve with soup. You can obviously make crostini with stale bread but I find them so useful that I tend to make batches with a fresh ciabatta loaf. Simply cut the bread on the diagonal into thin, even slices, spray or drizzle lightly with olive oil, and bake in a preheated oven at 350°F for 15 minutes until crisp. Let cool and store in an airtight container for up to 1 week. Topped with a light, moussey young goat or sheep's cheese and a sprinkling of herbs they make an attractive alternative to a slice of bread for a fresh vegetable soup (I find that crostini work particularly well with pea and broccoli soup).

For croutons, cut your bread into smaller pieces (unless you're making them for French Onion Soup on page 98) and bake them longer until they are hard, otherwise they'll go soggy when they hit the hot liquid or come into contact with melted cheese.

You could also serve miniature Welsh rarebits (grated Cheddar mixed with a little flour and English mustard powder, melted into a couple of spoonfuls of beer, and seasoned with black pepper and a dash of Worcestershire sauce—see page 146 for regular-size Welsh Rarebits). You can cut any kind of cheese toast into fingers—a nice accompaniment to winter vegetable soups, such as carrot, cauliflower, and pumpkin or butternut squash. With a stash of crostini and croutons and a hunk of cheese in your fridge, you'll always have the makings of a delicious snack.

CHEESE ALFRESCO

Just as wintertime has its own special cheese dishes (see Après-ski Cheese and Festive Cheese on pages 79 and 83 respectively), so some cheeses are perfectly suited to summer and outdoor eating.

In general, it's the younger, fresher cheeses that suit summer best. Top of the list in my book are **goat cheese** and **Feta** because they're so good with summer produce, particularly broiled vegetables such as bell peppers, zucchini, and eggplant. A platter of vegetables topped with crumbled cheese, drizzled with oil, and scattered with chopped fresh mint makes a perfect opener for a barbecue.

BROILED AND MELTED CHEESE

There are also cheeses you can actually broil. The most widely available one is the Greek and Cypriot cheese **Halloumi**, which keeps its shape even when exposed to an open fire. Marinate it in herb-infused oil, then broil it in slices (a useful meat substitute for vegetarians) or cut it into cubes and thread it on skewers with vegetables such as zucchini, bell peppers, and onions or simply with bay leaves, to create vegetarian kabobs. The Greek cheese **Kasseri** can be used in a similar way.

Other cheeses can be melted over broiled meat, such as burgers and steaks, to delicious effect, adding a slightly smoky taste to your favorite cheeseburger. **Taleggio** and milder **Gorgonzolas** (known as **Gorgonzola dolce** or **Dolcelatte**) are particularly good for this.

LEFT Barbecued Halloumi and bay leaf kabobs

PICNIC CHEESE

If you're taking cheese on a picnic, it's better to avoid the more pungent types and keep it simple. A medium-matured, not-too-runny **Brie** with a baguette and a bagful of cherries is a lovely picnic treat. **Camembert** works well too, as does a good-quality cream cheese, which you can transport in its own pot (delicious with peaches and nectarines).

An alternative—and a good one—is to incorporate the cheese element of the meal in a finished dish, such as a quiche (e.g. the Leek and Blue Cheese Quiche with Hazelnut Crust on page 115) or a flavored bread of the type the French call "cake" (e.g. the Quick Zucchini, Feta, and Mint Bread on page 132). Both are also good components of a casual alfresco supper. You can cut the "cake" up into cubes and hand it round with drinks, as many French hosts do.

Labneh with Herbs, Raw Vegetables, and Flatbread on page 140 also makes a fresh and healthy grazing plate for an outdoor meal, as does a light cheese dip with a selection of raw vegetables.

CHEESE-BASED SALADS

These make an easy and appealing warm-weather appetizer or, scaled up, attractive platters for a summer buffet. Try the Feta, Cucumber, and Mint, and Heirloom Tomato, Burrata, and Basil salads on page 94. Or for a simple family supper on the patio, try the delicious summery Zucchini, Mint, and Goat Cheese Soup on page 98.

CHEESE TIP

Pack it carefully! Cheese is a highly perishable food, so if you're taking it on a picnic you should obviously take care to transport it in a cool bag. Softer cheeses can easily squash and lose their shape so make sure they are well wrapped (preferably not in plastic wrap, which can make them "sweaty") or transported in a plastic box. And once you have unpacked it, keep it in the shade so that it remains cool and fresh. Personally, I wouldn't take a very smelly cheese on a picnic—it's amazing how its aroma can permeate a car, even from the trunk!

CHEESE AND WINE PARTIES

It must be at least 40 years ago now that cheese and wine parties were all the rage. You can see why—they were a simple way to entertain. No cooking, just a bit of cutting up. And the cheese was so bland that by and large there was never any problem serving red wine.

Maybe it's time to revisit these parties now that the range of cheeses open to us is greater, and of much higher quality than ever before. But let's update them and give them a stylish spin.

Over the next few pages you'll find a few ideas inspired by cheeses from other countries, but here are four suggestions that should impress your cheese-loving guests.

Cheddar and Cracked Pepper Straws, and Champagne

CHEESE AND WINE "STATIONS"

This is a great way to enjoy wine and cheese together and learn a little in the process. Set up four to six tables around the room, depending how much room you have, each with a different style of cheese and a different wine and some accompanying crackers and/or bread. They could include:

♦ A **goat cheese** with **Sauvignon Blanc** (it's always good to have at least a couple of cheeses for those who are intolerant to cow's milk)

♦ A **Brie-** or **Camembert-style** cheese with a fruity **Beaujolais** or **Pinot Noir**

♦ A **Cheddar** with an oaked **Chardonnay** and a **Merlot** (it will be interesting for your guests to see how the two compare)

♦ A **hard sheep's cheese** with a **Rioja** or other **Tempranillo-based red**

♦ A washed-rind cheese, such as **Munster** with a **Gewurztraminer**

♦ A **blue cheese** with **port** (for **Stilton**, for example, see the many other drink pairings on page 47). You could, of course, carry out a similar exercise with different beers and cheeses. Check out the recommended matches on page 42. Or surprise guests with an apple-flavored drinks and cheese evening based on the pairings on pages 40–41.

CHEESE AND CHAMPAGNE PARTY

Well, it doesn't have to be **Champagne** —a cheaper kind of fizz would be fine— but sparkling wine does go surprisingly well with cheese, particularly cheese pastries and crackers.

You could lay on a range of different canapés, such as gougères (cheese-flavored choux puffs); Cheddar and Cracked Pepper Straws (see page 136), or other little crisp cheese crackers or tartlets made with cheese pastry dough; individual quiches (make miniature versions of the Leek and Blue Cheese Quiche with Hazelnut Crust on page 115); mini cheese muffins (scale down the Double Cheese and Bacon Muffins on page 131); crostini topped with cheese; and mini-sandwiches or blinis topped with cream cheese and smoked salmon. (There is no reason why you should make all these yourself. You can buy excellent cheese crackers these days, for example.)

A CHEESE-THEMED DINNER PARTY

Your guests will be amazed at how different each course will taste. Kick off with one of the nibbles above, then you could serve the Parmesan Custards (see page 91) or one of the cheese salads on pages 94–95, steak with balsamic onions and molten blue cheese or roast lamb with Mushroom Dauphinois (see page 123), and the Lemon and Blueberry Upside-down Cheesecakes (see page 128), pairing each course with a matching wine—refer to the suggestions under individual recipes.

A MAC 'N' CHEESE 'N' WINE SUPPER

Serve the two mac and cheese recipes on page 120 and a choice of red and white wine. A fun and frugal evening!

See also the suggestions in Cutting Your Cheese Calories on page 153.

RIGHT *A cheese and wine station featuring Brie, glasses of Pinot Noir, and baguettes*

ROUND-THE-WORLD CHEESE

We tend to think of cheese as coming from the great cheese-producing nations of the world—France and Italy—but many other countries have a thriving cheese culture, such as the USA, Greece, Spain, Portugal, Mexico, and Australia. Here are some simple ideas for internationally themed cheese events.

CHEESE TAPAS

This is possibly one of the easiest themes to organize since tapas ingredients are so widely available these days. A very simple get-together for a drink could involve some fine slices of **Manchego** with membrillo (quince paste), sliced chorizo, Marcona almonds, and green olives with glasses of fresh **manzanilla sherry** (see picture opposite).

For a more substantial meal, you could add the Bell Pepper and Manchego Spanish Omelet on page 102, red bell peppers stuffed with goat cheese, or some *croquetas* (crisp little deep-fried rissoles with a creamy, cheesy filling). There are also other interesting Spanish cheeses to explore, including **Majorero** from the Canary Islands, and two powerful blues, **Valdeón** and **Cabrales**, which you could pair with sweet sherry and raisins.

CHEESE SMØRREBRØD

Cheese is not the central component of the traditional Danish and Norwegian smørrebrød table but makes an enjoyable addition to the usual fish- and meat-based offerings. Use your imagination (and the ideas on page 64) to create open sandwiches using Scandinavian cheeses, such as **Jarlsberg**, **Havarti**, **Samso**, and **Danish Blue**. You could try **cream cheese** topped with smoked salmon and cod roe, a slice of **Samso** topped with smoked beef or ham, finely sliced raw onions and pickles, and **Danish Blue** with figs.

Alternatively, lay out a selection of platters of different meats, cheeses, and salads for a traditional Swedish-style smorgasbord (which is essentially a buffet-style table of savory dishes). Miniaturized versions of the cheese and cucumber verrines on page 88 would fit in particularly well with this. **Beer** and **aquavit** are traditional accompaniments.

CHEESE ANTIPASTI

Again, this is a very simple way of entertaining at short notice. A selection of preserved broiled vegetables, such as artichokes, mushrooms, and bell peppers, with Parma or San Daniele ham, **Mozzarella** balls, ciabatta, and breadsticks makes a delicious, impromptu feast (see picture on page 77). Serve with a crisp, dry Italian white, such as **Pinot Grigio** from the Alto Adige, a **Prosecco**, or a lightly chilled **Valpolicella**.

If you wanted to add a couple of hot dishes, you could serve some *arancini* (deep-fried risotto balls) and *pizzette* (mini-pizzas) or, of course, go on to a pasta course.

LEFT *Classic tapas: Manchego with membrillo (quince paste), chorizo, Marcona almonds, green olives, and manzanilla sherry*

BEER AND BURRITOS

Beer and burritos is a great idea for a Mexican-themed evening. All you have to do is provide the ingredients for the burritos (see the recipe on page 109 for guidance) and let people make their own. As well as the ubiquitous **Sol**, there are some good Mexican beers around in specialist stores, such as **Negra Modelo**, a dark, flavorful beer.

For a shorter, more impromptu get-together, serve **margaritas** and *quesadillas*—little pan-fried cheese sandwiches made with tortillas. You can vary the filling by making them with ham, refried beans (see page 109), or simply with chopped jalapeño peppers. Cheese *empanadas*, which are popular throughout Central and South America, are also delicious but slightly more time-consuming to make.

CHEESE MEZZE OR MEZEDES

Serve homemade Labneh (see page 140) with fresh herbs, dukkah, and flatbread or with raw vegetables, such as carrots, cucumber, and celery, olives and pickled chiles for a light, Middle Eastern-inspired meal. Wine wouldn't be traditional with this kind of food; you could serve **beer** and **raki** (or **ouzo**) but might also want to offer a soft drink like **pomegranate juice**.

The Greeks have a similar tradition of small plates called "mezedes," which might include preserved **Feta** or deep-fried or broiled **Kasseri** or **Kefalotyri** cheese served with a squeeze of lemon. You could add some taramasalata, broiled or preserved octopus, stuffed vine leaves or *gigantes*, the tasty butter beans in tomato sauce. If you wanted a more substantial course, add some wedges of *spanakopita*, Greece's famous spinach and Feta pie. Again, **ouzo** or **beer** would be traditional accompaniments but there are such good Greek wines around now that it would be a shame not to try one. I'd serve a crisp **Assyrtiko**.

A LATE-NIGHT FRENCH BISTRO SUPPER

Follow the example of Parisian party-goers who used to go to Les Halles in the early hours of the morning for sustaining bowlfuls of onion soup, topped with slices of broiled country bread and melted cheese (see recipe on page 98). It's a great finale to an evening at the theatre or a cold outdoor sporting event. A simple dry white wine (**Aligoté** is traditional), some crusty bread, and a leafy green salad make perfect accompaniments. Finish the meal off with a classic French fruit tart. (See also Après-ski Cheese overleaf.)

RIGHT *Cheese antipasti: Mozzarella balls with preserved broiled artichokes, mushrooms, and bell peppers, Parma ham, and breadsticks*

APRES-SKI CHEESE

Even if you don't go skiing, you can't fail to be captivated by the traditional après-ski hot cheese dishes that are served up after a day on the slopes. I can't think of better dishes to welcome friends round on a cold winter evening than deliciously, meltingly gooey fondue, raclette, and tartiflette.

With all of these melted cheese dishes, it pays to use the best, authentic ingredients. **Fondue** is probably the best known—and the hardest to get right until you've made it a couple of times (a bit like learning to swim or ride a bicycle!) You can find a recipe on page 106 (made with hard cider, which works just as well as white wine) but the key points to bear in mind are: make sure your cheese (usually **Gruyère** and **Emmental**) is at room temperature; take the pan off the heat before you start adding the cheese; and stir with a figure-eight rather than a circular motion, which can cause the cheese to ball up and separate from the liquid. In order to keep control of the process, it's best to make it for a small group—no more than six—unless you have a couple of fondue sets and an extra pair of hands to supervise the second batch.

Raclette, which is of Swiss origin and the name of both the cheese and the dish, is better for a larger group. You can buy or hire a purpose-made raclette maker, which may either consist of a number of small pans or a more complicated grill-like mechanism into which you wedge the cheese, pass it directly under the heat, and shear the molten cheese off into a dish of boiled new potatoes garnished with pearl onions and pickles. You can also offer some air-dried country ham and sliced vegetables, such as zucchini and bell peppers, to eat with the molten cheese.

Tartiflette (see recipe on page 112), which comes from the Savoie region of France, is probably the most straightforward of the three dishes. It's a wickedly rich bake of potatoes, onions, bacon, and **Reblochon** cheese quite similar in style to a gratin dauphinois. It makes a great winter supper dish with a green salad.

You could also incorporate an "après-ski" element to your winter entertaining by serving a **Vacherin**, one of my all-time favorite cheeses. It goes by different names depending on which side of the Alps it's made—France or Switzerland—but is generally marketed as **Vacherin Mont d'Or** or **Vacherin du Haut-Doubs** (see page 18). It comes in a box and looks a bit like a giant Camembert with an undulating pinkish rind but it has a wonderfully unctuous creamy interior. You can either serve it at room temperature or bake it in its box for a fonduelike effect. Again, new potatoes (sprinkled with crunchy sea salt) are an excellent accompaniment.

Note that red wine tends to be positively unpleasant with all these dishes. A **crisp, fruity dry white** is infinitely preferable, or even, in the case of **Vacherin**, a glass of **Champagne**.

LEFT *Baked Vacherin Mont d'Or with boiled new potatoes and sea salt*

FESTIVE CHEESE

The time of year when we all want to put on a particularly spectacular cheese offering is the Thanksgiving and Christmas holiday period. And that's as much about dressing up your board and the other ingredients you pick as the cheeses you choose.

I like to create a colorful cheese board full of warm, rich colors by mixing the traditional accompaniments of satsumas, clementines, and nuts with some of the fabulous products you can now buy at any supermarket or deli counter: big lush raisins, fresh Medjool dates (instead of the oversweet, sticky preserved ones of my youth), slices of delicious Spanish fig roll, a few candied pecans, even some pieces of brilliant orange dried mango or a rosy pomegranate all look fabulously festive.

Blue cheese is, of course, traditional for Christmas but it could just as well be a rich **Rogue River Blue** as a **Stilton**. Partner it with a fine, golden **Fiscalini Cheddar** from California, a brilliant orange-rinded cheese, such as a **Stinking Bishop** or French **Epoisses**, and a deep orange **Mimolette** from Northern France and you've echoed those rich colors in your cheese board too—almost like a classic Dutch still life.

You can also create pretty seasonal cheese plates with these ingredients— hunt around for gold plates (often to be found in cheap chain or party stores).

OTHER IDEAS FOR THANKSGIVING AND CHRISTMAS

◆ For a Christmas twist on a classic English cream tea, bake a batch of scones and fill them with **cream cheese** and cranberry sauce instead of cream and jam. You could also offer some **Parmesan** scones or mini cheese muffins studded with dried cranberries.

◆ For a quick snack, halve baguettes lengthwise and fill with sliced **Brie** and cranberry sauce or use the same ingredients to top crostini for a quick and easy canapé. (Leftover holiday cheese can also be whizzed into a tasty cheese spread for crostini toppings— see page 146.)

◆ For those who are sated with sweet things, finish a meal with a scoop or two of **Stilton** with some toasted walnut bread, some jewel-red Spiced Quince Compote with Red Wine and Cloves (see page 145), and a glass of **port**

◆ For a show-stopping "cheesert," take a small whole **Brie**, carefully slice the rind off the top, and spread with a thick cranberry, raspberry, and cherry compote. Serve it in wedges, like a cheesecake.

◆ Make Christmas **mascarpone** "trifles" similar to the Lemon and Blueberry Upside-down Cheesecakes on page 128: start with a compote like the one above—laced with a dash of **cherry brandy** if you have some—a vanilla-flavored mascarpone topping, and a scattering of caramelized pine nuts

HALLOWE'EN CHEESE

Hallowe'en is becoming such a major celebration in its own right that it deserves its own cheese board. It would have to be largely orange, as there aren't any black cheeses I'm aware of, although you could serve an **ash-coated goat cheese** or a **black wax-coated Cheddar** and have some

ready-to-eat prunes and charcoal crackers on the side. (Hallowe'en is nothing if not kitsch!) Perfect candidates for orange cheeses would be **Mimolette**, as described above, a washed-rind cheese, such as **Epoisses** or **Stinking Bishop** (the idea of a stinky cheese seems particularly suitable for Hallowe'en, I feel), and **Red Leicester** from England. You could even carry the black—or near black—and orange theme through to the drinks. **Port** and **elderberry wine** are pretty dark in color or try a **pumpkin ale**.

CHEESE TIP

Although nuts in general are a good partner for cheese, there are specific pairings that stand out, for example walnuts and pecans (candied or uncoated) with blue cheeses, such as Gorgonzola or Cashel Blue; almonds with sheep's cheeses, such as Manchego; Brazil nuts with cream cheese; and hazelnuts with goat cheese.

LEFT *Mimolette with Medjool dates, dried figs, nuts, and tawny port*
PAGES 80–81 *Shropshire Blue, Epoisses, Mimolette, clementines, raisins, fresh Medjool dates, slices of Spanish fig roll, fresh pomegranate, and port*

COOKING
WITH CHEESE

COOKING WITH CHEESE

Most of us, I suspect, get stuck in a rut when it comes to using cheese in cooking. If we need a hard grating cheese, it's Parmesan; for a fondue, Gruyère; for a sauce, Cheddar; for a salad, a goat cheese or a crumbly blue. But there are, as I hope you'll discover over the next few pages, many other possibilities.

The main thing to get out of your mind when cooking with cheese is that it's somehow "a waste" to use a good cheese for cooking, in much the same way that people think they shouldn't use a decent wine. No one would think that about meat or fish. You get out of a dish what you put into it in terms of quality. Moreover, using stronger, more intensely flavored cheeses means you can use less of them, which makes for healthier recipes (see page 153) and a lighter-textured dish.

Of course cheese is an expensive ingredient and you wouldn't necessarily want to cook with a rare and special cheese you've bought to savor in its own right. But it's surprising the effect you can achieve by using top-quality cheese on a pizza (see page 111) or a washed-rind cheese, such as **Reblochon** or **Taleggio** (one of my favorite cooking cheeses), in a tart. And it's a valuable way of using up the last remnants of a fine cheese that might otherwise go to waste.

There may also be uses for cheeses you might not have thought of. Baking a whole **Camembert**, for example, is an easy way of producing an instant fondue. Lightly flour slices of **Mozzarella di bufala** and fry them for quick, delicious cheese fritters. Marinate **Halloumi** with olive oil and herbs and grill it on the barbecue. Make crisp little cheese crisps from grated Cheddar (see page 120) and use them to make the ultimate Extra-crispy Macaroni and

Cheese (also on page 120). Mix **mascarpone** with lemon curd for an instant and indulgent dessert (see page 128). Even making your own cheese is child's play, as you'll see if you try the easy recipe for the delicious Middle Eastern cheese labneh (see page 140).

You'll get the best results from the cheese you use if you follow a few general guidelines. In general, it's better to cut off the rind, certainly on well-matured, hard cheeses, such as **Cheddar**, although there are exceptions, such as in Tartiflette (see page 112) where the rind of the **Reblochon** really contributes to the flavor of the finished dish.

If you are grating cheese or trying to shave fine slices, it's easier to do this with cheese that's just been taken out of the refrigerator, although for some recipes, such as fondue (see page 106), you will need to bring the cheese to room temperature before using it. And, with the exception of fondue, don't cook cheese too long over a direct heat or it can develop a stringy texture. Cheese is best added to a sauce once it's been taken off the heat.

CHEESES FOR MELTING

Gruyère, Emmental, Fontina, Cheddar

CHEESES FOR GRATINS

Parmesan, Grana Padano, Pecorino

CHEESES FOR PIZZA

Mozzarella, Taleggio, Gorgonzola (if you fancy a blue)

CHEESES FOR SALADS

Young **goat cheeses**, crumbly white cheeses, such as **Caerphilly**, crumbly blues, such as **Stilton**. Shaveable cheeses, such as **Parmesan** and **Pecorino** also work well.

CHEESES FOR DESSERTS

Ricotta, mascarpone

CHEESE AND CUCUMBER VERRINES

"Verrines" are all the rage in France—stylish little appetizers or desserts that are layered in a glass. Here are two variations on a theme, based on the very complementary ingredients of cucumber and soft cheese. The two verrines look fantastic together at a summer supper party or buffet. Serve a crisp, dry Riesling with both.

CUCUMBER AND RICOTTA VERRINES WITH SHRIMP

2 cucumbers, peeled

1 envelope powdered gelatin

3 tablespoons lowfat milk

8 oz. ricotta

⅔ cup lowfat yogurt

2 tablespoons finely chopped fresh dill leaves, plus several sprigs to garnish

2 teaspoons strained lemon juice, plus extra lemon juice to season the shrimp

5 oz. cooked, peeled shrimp

sea salt and white pepper

6–8 tumblers or small glass dishes

SERVES 6–8

Cut the cucumbers in half lengthwise and scoop out the seeds with the tip of a teaspoon. Halve lengthwise again, then cut each piece into 3 long strips and cut across into small dice. Put in a colander and sprinkle with salt. Leave for about 20 minutes.

Sprinkle the gelatin over 3 tablespoons cold water in a small dish. Let dissolve for 5 minutes. Meanwhile, gently heat the milk in a small saucepan until almost boiling. When the gelatin has dissolved, pour it into the warm milk. Remove from the heat and stir until well mixed.

Put the ricotta and yogurt in a food processor and whizz until smooth. Tip into a bowl, scraping the food processor bowl thoroughly with a rubber spatula. Stir in the milk and gelatin, the dill, and lemon juice. Rinse the cucumber with cold water and pat dry. Fold just over half the cucumber into the ricotta mixture and season with salt to taste. Divide the mixture between the tumblers, cover, and refrigerate for 2 hours to set. Cover the remaining cucumber and refrigerate too.

Scatter the creams with the remaining cucumber and top with shrimp. Squeeze over a little lemon juice and decorate with dill.

CUCUMBER AND FROMAGE FRAIS VERRINES WITH SMOKED SALMON

1 envelope powdered gelatin

1¼ cups light vegetable stock (use ⅓ bouillon cube or 1 teaspoon bouillon powder)

freshly squeezed juice of 1 lime

1 teaspoon sugar

2 medium/large cucumbers, peeled

3 tablespoons finely snipped fresh chives, plus extra to garnish

6½ oz. fromage frais, quark, or other fresh cheese

2–3 tablespoons lowfat milk

4 oz. wafer-thin smoked salmon, cut into strips

sea salt and white pepper

6–8 tumblers or small glass dishes

SERVES 6–8

Sprinkle the gelatin over 3 tablespoons cold water in a small dish. Let dissolve for 5 minutes.

Pour the vegetable stock into a small saucepan with the lime juice and sugar and heat until almost boiling. When the gelatin has dissolved, pour it into the pan. Remove from the heat and stir until well mixed, then strain into a measuring cup and set aside to cool.

Cut the cucumbers in half lengthwise and scoop out the seeds with the tip of a teaspoon. Halve lengthwise again, then cut each piece into 3 long strips and cut across into small dice. Put in a colander and sprinkle with salt. Leave for about 20 minutes, then rinse with cold water and pat dry. Mix with the chives. Half-fill the tumblers with the cucumber and pour over enough cooled stock to cover. Cover and refrigerate for at least 1½ hours to set.

When the jelly is firm, mix the fromage frais with enough milk to make a soft, spoonable consistency, season, and spoon a layer over the jelly. Top with smoked salmon and decorate with chives.

PARMESAN CUSTARDS WITH ANCHOVY TOASTS

A delectable appetizer that has probably been one of the most popular recipes of the past year since Rowley Leigh added it to the menu of his London restaurant, Le Café Anglais. I keep meaning to order something different but never manage to.

1¼ cups light cream
1¼ cups whole milk
1 cup finely grated Parmesan
4 egg yolks
cayenne pepper
12 anchovy fillets
3 tablespoons unsalted butter
8 very thin slices of rustic loaf
sea salt and finely ground white pepper

8 x ⅓-cup ramekins or ovenproof dishes, buttered

SERVES 8

Mix the cream, milk, and all but 1 tablespoon of the Parmesan in a heatproof bowl, place it over a saucepan of boiling water, and warm it gently until the Parmesan has melted. Remove the bowl from on top of the pan and let cool completely.

Preheat the oven to 300°F.

Whisk the egg yolks, a pinch of salt, a pinch of white pepper, and a little cayenne pepper into the cool cream mixture, then pour into the prepared ramekins. Place the ramekins in an ovenproof dish in the oven, then pour boiling water from the kettle into the dish to reach halfway up the ramekins. Cover the whole dish with a sheet of buttered parchment paper and bake in the preheated oven for 15 minutes or until the custards have just set. Remove from the oven and turn on the broiler.

Mash the anchovies and butter to make a smooth paste and spread over 4 of the slices of bread. Cover with the remaining bread and toast in a sandwich maker or panini machine. Sprinkle the remaining Parmesan over the warm custards and brown gently under the hot broiler. Cut the toasted anchovy sandwiches into fingers and serve alongside the custards.

What to drink: Champagne is a great pairing with Parmesan but you could serve any similar dry sparkling wine.

LEFT Parmesan Custards with Anchovy Toasts

ICEBERG LETTUCE WEDGES WITH BLUE CHEESE DRESSING

This is a great side dish for a burger or steak. Don't be tempted to whizz the dressing ingredients together otherwise it will turn an ugly grayish-green.

1 small/medium iceberg lettuce

DRESSING
2 tablespoons white wine vinegar or cider vinegar
2 tablespoons extra virgin olive oil
⅓ cup grapeseed oil
2 tablespoons heavy or whipping cream
1½ oz. crumbly blue cheese, e.g. Stilton, Maytag Blue, or Fourme d'Ambert
3 scallions, trimmed and very finely chopped
freshly squeezed lemon juice, to taste
sea salt and freshly ground black pepper

SERVES 4

First make the dressing. Whisk the vinegar with a little salt and pepper, then gradually whisk in the 2 oils. Finally, whisk in the cream. Roughly break up the blue cheese and add to the dressing, together with most of the scallions, leaving a little for garnish. Set the mixture aside for 15–30 minutes to allow the flavors to blend.

Remove any soft or damaged outer leaves from the lettuce, cut off the base, then cut the lettuce into 4 wedges. Soak in ice water for 10 minutes, then remove, shake off any excess water, and dry thoroughly with paper towels or a clean kitchen towel.

Taste the dressing again, adding more salt and pepper if you think it needs it, and a squeeze of lemon juice. Put a lettuce wedge on each plate, spoon over the dressing, and sprinkle with the remaining scallions.

Variation: You could use the same dressing with halved or quartered Bibb or Boston lettuces. It also works well with a spinach and raw mushroom salad.

What to drink: A white Burgundy or similar Chardonnay would be great with this.

THIS PAGE *Feta, Cucumber, and Mint Spring Salad*
RIGHT *Heirloom Tomato, Burrata, and Basil Summer Salad*

SEASONAL CHEESE SALADS

The perfect basis for a light lunch that can be varied from season to season.

FETA, CUCUMBER, AND MINT SPRING SALAD

A fabulously fresh-tasting summery salad that I discovered in one of my favorite London restaurants, Ransome's Dock, which in turn adapted it from a dish at Zuni Café in San Francisco!

2 mini-cucumbers
6 radishes
2 good handfuls of arugula
a small handful of fresh mint leaves
5 oz. Feta, broken into small pieces
10–15 small black olives

DRESSING
3 tablespoons extra virgin olive oil
1 tablespoon red wine vinegar
a good squeeze of lemon juice
sea salt and freshly ground black pepper

SERVES 2

To make the dressing, whisk or shake the ingredients together in a lidded jar.

Cut the cucumbers in half lengthwise and scoop out the seeds with the tip of a teaspoon. Slice lengthwise using a mandoline or vegetable peeler to make wafer-thin slices. Trim the radishes and thinly slice on the diagonal.

Put the arugula, mint, cucumber, and radishes in a bowl and toss together with the dressing. Add the crumbled Feta and toss lightly again, then scatter over the olives. Divide the ingredients between 2 plates, piling them up in a mound. Serve with ciabatta or other crusty bread.

What to drink: A crisp, fruity white or a dry rosé.

HEIRLOOM TOMATO, BURRATA, AND BASIL SUMMER SALAD

A deluxe version of the eternally popular tomato and Mozzarella salad using Burrata, a wonderful fresh cheese from Puglia which is based on Mozzarella and cream. A real high summer treat.

1 lb. mixed heirloom tomatoes in different colors
3–4 tablespoons fragrant, grassy extra virgin olive oil, plus extra to drizzle
10 oz. Burrata
leaves from 3 sprigs of fresh basil (purple basil, if possible)
balsamic vinegar, to drizzle
sea salt and freshly ground black pepper

SERVES 4

Remove the stalks from the tomatoes. Slice the larger ones and halve the smaller ones or leave them whole. Transfer to a bowl. Spoon over the olive oil, season with salt and pepper, toss together, and leave for 10 minutes.

Divide the tomatoes between 4 small plates. Roughly tear the Burrata into small chunks and distribute them over the tomatoes. Scatter with the basil leaves. Drizzle over a little more oil and some balsamic vinegar, and serve with crusty bread.

What to drink: A lightly oaked Sauvignon or a Sauvignon-Sémillon blend.

CHEESE, APPLE, AND HAZELNUT FALL SALAD

A pretty autumnal salad that is substantial enough to serve as an entrée.

2 tablespoons shelled hazelnuts
1 tablespoon sunflower oil
3½ oz. thick-sliced bacon or pancetta, cut into small cubes
1 Bibb or Boston lettuce, leaves separated
2½ oz. smoked chicken, torn into strips
2 oz. Comté or Beaufort (rind removed), thinly sliced on the diagonal
1 tart apple, quartered, cored, and cut into wedges
a few root vegetable crisps
a small handful of fresh chives, snipped

DRESSING
2 tablespoons crabapple jelly or red currant jelly
2 tablespoons pure apple juice
1 teaspoon cider vinegar
sea salt and freshly ground black pepper

SERVES 2

Preheat the oven to 350°F.

Put the hazelnuts on a baking sheet and roast in the preheated oven for 10 minutes, or until the skins turn dark brown. Let cool for a few minutes, then tip them onto a clean kitchen towel and rub off the skins. Cut the hazelnuts in half.

Heat the oil in a skillet and fry the bacon until crisp. Take the skillet off the heat, remove the bacon from the skillet with a slotted spoon, and transfer to a plate lined with paper towels. Pour off all but 1 tablespoon of the fat, add the crabapple jelly for the dressing, and stir until melted, putting the skillet back on the heat if necessary. Add the apple juice and cider vinegar, and a splash of water if needed to thin the dressing. Season with salt and pepper and set aside.

Take 2 plates and arrange the lettuce leaves on each plate. Top with the bacon and smoked chicken, then the cheese and apple. Drizzle over the dressing and scatter with the hazelnuts, a few root vegetable crisps, and the chives. Serve the remaining root vegetable crisps in a bowl alongside or offer some crusty bread.

What to drink: A glass of cider or lightly oaked Chenin Blanc or Chardonnay. A fruity red, such as a Pinot Noir, would work too.

STICHELTON AND STEAK WINTER SALAD WITH ONIONS AND ARUGULA

Stichelton is a wonderful new unpasteurized blue that is made to a similar recipe to Stilton (which you can easily substitute). A very easy and stylish dinner for two.

8 oz. lean steak, trimmed of any fat
extra virgin olive oil
1 onion, thinly sliced
about 1 tablespoon balsamic vinegar
½ cup cherry tomatoes
2 handfuls of arugula
2 oz. Stichelton or Stilton, rind removed
sea salt and freshly ground black pepper

SERVES 2

Lay the steak on a sheet of parchment paper on a cutting board, cover with another sheet of parchment paper, and beat out with a meat mallet or rolling pin. Rub a little olive oil into both sides of the steak and season lightly with salt and pepper. Heat a ridged stovetop griddle pan until almost smoking, then lay the steak in the pan and cook for 1 minute. Turn and cook for 1 minute on the other side, then transfer from the pan to a plate.

Turn down the heat under the pan slightly, smear a little oil over the onion slices, and place them in a single layer in the pan. Cook for a couple of minutes until beginning to turn dark brown, then carefully turn and cook the other side. Set aside on another plate and drizzle over a little of the balsamic vinegar.

Finally, tip the cherry tomatoes into the pan with a little extra oil, if necessary, and roll them around until the skins begin to burst.

Cut the steak into fine slices with a sharp knife. Divide the arugula between 2 plates, top with the onions, and arrange the tomatoes round the plate. Scatter over the steak slices and crumble over the Stichelton. Trickle over a little extra oil and balsamic vinegar and season with pepper. This salad is good with a crusty baguette, warm ciabatta, or a baked potato.

What to drink: You might be surprised, given that red wine and blue cheese aren't generally the most accommodating of partners, but a fruity Cabernet Sauvignon will go well with this. (The steak and onions counteract the slight bitterness of the cheese.)

THIS PAGE *Cheese, Apple, and Hazelnut Fall Salad*
RIGHT *Stichelton and Steak Winter Salad with Onions and Arugula*

ZUCCHINI, MINT, AND GOAT CHEESE SOUP

Cheese can be used both to add richness and texture to a soup, and also as a flavorful topping. This deliciously light, summery soup combines both uses. You could vary the recipe by including broccoli or even peas, or substituting dill for the mint.

3 tablespoons olive oil

a small bunch of scallions, trimmed and sliced

1 small/medium potato, thinly sliced

1 lb. small/medium zucchini

2 sprigs of fresh mint

3 cups vegetable stock (use a bouillon cube or 1 tablespoon bouillon powder)

2 tablespoons butter

4 oz. young, crumbly goat cheese

sea salt and freshly ground black pepper

SERVES 4

Heat the oil in a heavy saucepan, then add the scallions and potato. Stir, cover with a lid, reduce the heat, and cook over low heat for about 7–8 minutes or until the potato starts to soften. Slice 1 of the zucchini and add to the pan along with the mint stalks (chop the leaves finely and set aside). Stir and cook for 1–2 minutes, then add 2 cups of the stock. Bring to a boil, then simmer until the potatoes are cooked (about 15–20 minutes). Meanwhile, grate the remaining zucchini and drain them in a colander, pressing them gently to extract any liquid.

Heat a large skillet and add the butter. When the butter stops foaming, tip in the grated zucchini and stir-fry for about 1 minute. Add the chopped mint leaves, fry for another 30 seconds, then set aside. Once the potatoes are tender, take the soup off the heat, remove the mint stalks, and tip in three-quarters of the grated zucchini mixture. Whizz the soup in batches in a food processor, returning the puréed soup to a clean pan. Pour the remaining stock into the food processor to collect the remnants of the vegetable purée and pour into the soup. Reheat the soup to boiling point and take off the heat. Crumble in just under half the goat cheese and whisk to blend. Season to taste.

Quickly reheat the remaining grated zucchini mixture. Ladle the soup into warm bowls, scatter a little grated zucchini over the top, and crumble over the remaining goat cheese.

What to drink: Sauvignon Blanc or apple juice.

FRENCH ONION SOUP

French onion soup is one of the classic bistro dishes, made luxuriant by its cheese and bread topping. Like many simple recipes it needs good ingredients. The critical thing to remember is to cook the onions long enough and to use a substantial, densely textured bread, preferably a couple of days old.

1 sourdough baguette or other long rustic loaf

2 tablespoons olive oil

3 tablespoons butter

2–3 large mild onions (about 1½ lbs. in total), thinly sliced

½ teaspoon sugar

½ teaspoon dried thyme

a glass of dry white wine (about ⅔ cup)

5 cups beef, chicken, or vegetable stock (made with 2 organic bouillon cubes)

white wine vinegar, to taste (optional)

4 oz. Gruyère (rind removed), coarsely grated

sea salt and freshly ground black pepper

SERVES 4

Preheat the oven to 350°F. Cut the bread into slices about 1 inch thick and lay on a baking sheet. Bake in the preheated oven for 15–20 minutes or until crisp and lightly browned, then set aside. (You can do this ahead when you have the oven on.)

Heat the oil in a large ovenproof casserole dish, add the butter, and tip in the onions. Stir so that they're thoroughly coated with oil and cook over low/medium heat, stirring them occasionally, until they go a rich, deep brown. This may take up to 40 minutes, depending on your onions. Add the sugar, if using, once they start to brown, and stir more regularly—you don't want to burn them. Once the onions are a good color, stir in the thyme and wine and let it bubble up and reduce by half. Add the stock, bring back to a boil, and simmer for about 20–25 minutes. Check for seasoning, adding salt and pepper to taste and a few drops of vinegar if you think it tastes too sweet. Preheat the broiler.

Ladle the soup into 4 individual ovenproof bowls. Lay the slices of bread over the surface of the soup, pressing them down lightly. Scatter over the Gruyère and broil for 5–10 minutes until bubbling.

What to drink: Traditionally, the French would drink a crisp, dry white like an Aligoté with this kind of dish.

RIGHT French Onion Soup

GOAT CHEESE OMELET WITH WILD GARLIC AND CHERVIL

This is a recipe prompted by a spring visit to the farmers' market. If you haven't had goat cheese in an omelet before, do try it—it has a surprising affinity with eggs.

a small handful of fresh chervil or parsley
2 large or 3 medium eggs
2 wild garlic leaves, finely shredded,
or some finely snipped fresh chives
1 tablespoon butter
½ oz. goat cheese, crumbled
sea salt and freshly ground black pepper

SERVES 1

Pick over the chervil, cutting away the tougher stems, and chop finely. Beat the eggs in a bowl with a splash of water (about 1 tablespoon), add the chopped chervil and wild garlic leaves, and beat again. Season lightly with salt and pepper.

Heat a medium skillet or omelet pan until hot, add the butter, swirl it round, and pour in the beaten eggs and herbs, swirling them around the skillet. Lift the edge of the omelet as it begins to cook, letting the liquid egg run from the center to the edge. Scatter over the goat cheese and leave for a minute to allow the omelet to brown. Add more pepper if you like. Fold one side of the omelet over and tip it onto a plate. You could serve this with some lightly dressed mixed salad leaves.

What to drink: A glass of smooth, dry white wine, such as an Alsace Pinot Blanc or an unoaked Chardonnay would pair well with this.

BUCKWHEAT GALETTES WITH PROSCIUTTO AND EMMENTAL

These are based on the delicious dark buckwheat flour crêpes you find in Brittany and crêperies all over France, but they have been given a bit of an Italian twist with the inclusion of prosciutto and olive oil.

½ cup buckwheat flour
½ cup all-purpose flour
½ teaspoon salt
2 large eggs
4 tablespoons olive oil
3 tablespoons butter
12 thin slices of prosciutto or other air-dried ham
1½ cups grated Emmental
freshly ground black pepper

MAKES 6–8 LARGE PANCAKES

Put the 2 flours, the salt, eggs, and half the oil in a food processor with ⅔ cup water. Whizz until smooth, then gradually add another ⅔ cup water so that you have a thin batter. Process for another minute, then let rest for 10 minutes. Alternatively, you can make the batter by hand with a whisk and a large bowl.

Gently melt 1 tablespoon of the butter with the remaining oil in a small saucepan and set aside. Heat a pancake pan or skillet until moderately hot but not smoking. Pour in a little of the melted butter and oil and spread over the pan with a paper towel. Pour in the batter with a ladle, tipping the pan as you do so, so that the batter runs quickly and evenly over the surface. Cook for about 30 seconds until no uncooked mixture shows, then flip the pancake over and cook for a further 30 seconds. Slip the pancake onto a warm plate and make the next pancake, greasing the pan as you go.

Once you've made all the pancakes, place 2–3 pieces of ham on each one and sprinkle with a small handful of Emmental, season with pepper, and fold in half like a sandwich. Melt the remaining butter and pour a little into the pancake pan or skillet. Wipe with a paper towel. Heat the pancakes up 2 at a time, cooking on each side until they are crisp and the cheese has melted. Repeat with the remaining pancakes, greasing the pan between each batch, and serve straightaway with a green salad.

What to drink: A sparkling Normandy hard cider or still British hard cider would be delicious, or try a simple Vin Blanc.

LEFT *Goat Cheese Omelet with Wild Garlic and Chervil*

BELL PEPPER AND MANCHEGO SPANISH OMELET

The addition of cheese to an omelet makes it substantial enough for an entrée, as well as a stylish tapas dish. You may feel it's time-consuming to fry the vegetables separately but I find that it enormously improves the flavor and texture of the finished dish.

⅓ cup Spanish extra virgin olive oil, plus extra to fry

1 large Spanish onion (about 8 oz.), very thinly sliced

1 large, flavorful red bell pepper, quartered, seeded, and finely sliced (try to find field-grown peppers if possible; you can also use a couple of marinated roasted peppers, in which case add them at the same time as the Manchego)

12 oz. new potatoes, very thinly sliced

8 eggs

2½ oz. Manchego, thinly sliced

sea salt and freshly ground black pepper

a deep 9-inch skillet

SERVES 4–6

Heat ¼ cup of the oil in a large, deep lidded skillet or wok, then fry the onion and bell pepper over medium heat until soft and beginning to brown at the edges. Remove from the skillet with a slotted spoon, leaving behind the oil.

Add the remaining oil to the skillet, heat for 1 minute, then tip in the potatoes and stir with a spatula to ensure the slices are separate and well coated in oil. Fry, stirring, for about 5–6 minutes until they start to brown, then reduce the heat, cover with the lid, and cook for another 10–15 minutes until the potatoes are tender, turning them every so often so that they don't catch.

Tip the onion and pepper back into the skillet, mix with the potatoes, and continue to fry (uncovered) for another 5 minutes. Season generously with salt and pepper and set aside for 10 minutes or so to cool.

Break the eggs into a large bowl and beat lightly. Tip the contents of the skillet and the Manchego into the beaten eggs and mix gently. Heat your deep 9-inch skillet until moderately hot, add a little oil, wipe off the excess with a paper towel, then pour in the egg mixture. Lift the edge of the omelet as it begins to cook, letting the liquid egg run from the center to the edge. Cook until most of the egg has set, then reduce the heat a little and cook for about 3–4 minutes. Meanwhile, preheat the broiler to medium.

Slip the skillet under the broiler about 5 inches from the heat and leave until the top of the omelet has puffed up and lightly browned and the egg in the middle has set (about 4 minutes). Remove from under the broiler and let cool for about 30 minutes in the skillet, then loosen it round the edge. Place a plate over the skillet and flip the omelet over so that it lands bottom-side up. Cut into wedges and serve at room temperature.

What to drink: This makes a good addition to a tapas selection so you could have a glass of manzanilla sherry with it.

CHEESE AND BASIL SOUFFLES

Soufflés are one of the most impressive recipes you can make for your friends—guaranteed to provoke "oohs" and "aaahs" from everyone around the table, especially with this unusual combination of cheese and basil. They're not as difficult as they look—you just need to keep your nerve!

¾ cup whole milk

4–6 sprigs of fresh basil (depending how strong they are)

4 large eggs (or 5 if your whites are unusually small)

2 tablespoons butter

2 tablespoons all-purpose flour

½ cup grated mature Gruyère or sharp Cheddar

3 tablespoons freshly grated mature Parmesan, plus extra to dust the dish

sea salt and freshly ground black pepper

a 6-inch soufflé dish, 3½ inches high, lightly buttered

SERVES 4 AS AN APPETIZER OR 2 AS AN ENTREE

Put the milk in a saucepan, add the basil sprigs, and bring slowly to a boil. Turn the heat right down, simmer for 1 minute, then turn off the heat and leave the basil to infuse for about 20 minutes.

Separate the eggs carefully—put the whites in a large, clean bowl and set aside 3 of the yolks to add to the sauce.

Preheat the oven to 400°F.

Put a large, heavy-based saucepan over medium heat and add the butter. When that has melted, stir in the flour. Cook for a few seconds, then tip in the warm basil-infused milk through a strainer. Whisk together until smooth, then cook over low heat until thick.

Stir in the grated Gruyère and most of the Parmesan and put back over low heat until the cheese has melted. Let cool for 5 minutes. Stir in the 3 egg yolks one by one.

Sprinkle the inside of the buttered soufflé dish with a little Parmesan, shaking off any excess. Transfer to a baking sheet.

Whisk the egg whites and a pinch of salt until holding their shape but not stiff. Take 2 tablespoons of the whites and fold it into the cheese base, then carefully fold in the rest of the whites without overmixing. Tip the mixture into the prepared soufflé dish, scraping the last remnants in with a rubber spatula. Sprinkle with a little more Parmesan and bake in the preheated oven for 25–30 minutes until the soufflé is well risen and browned. (Don't open the oven door or your soufflé may collapse!) Serve immediately with some new potatoes or crusty bread and a green salad.

Variation: You can make these in individual ramekins, as shown opposite, if you prefer. In this case, bake them for 20–25 minutes.

What to drink: Champagne or other sparkling wines work extremely well with soufflés, or you could drink a smooth dry white, such as Chablis, Alsace Pinot Blanc, or Gavi di Gavi.

CHEDDAR AND CIDER FONDUE

Although the classic fondue recipe is Swiss, it's perfectly possible to make it with other cheeses. This one is one of my favorites, made from a selection of farmstead cheeses and Somerset hard cider. The key things to remember with fondue are to have your cheeses at room temperature before you start, to take the pan off the heat before adding the first batch of cheese, and to stir in a figure eight rather than round and round (which makes the fondue more likely to separate). Once you've got the knack, it's simplicity itself.

3 cups grated farmstead Cheddar and 4 oz. soft ripened farmstead cheese, such as Brie, Camembert, or California Teleme, rind removed

2 teaspoons cornstarch or potato flour

¾ cup dry but fruity hard cider

1 tablespoon apple brandy or Calvados

freshly ground white or black pepper

crusty whole-wheat or granary rolls, cubed, to serve

apple wedges, to serve

a cast-iron cheese fondue set

SERVES 2–3

Toss the cheese with the cornstarch. Set aside until it has come to room temperature.

Start off the fondue on the stovetop. Pour the cider into your fondue pan and heat until almost boiling. Remove from the heat and tip in about one-third of the cheese. Keep breaking up the cheese with a wooden spoon using a figure eight motion. (Stirring it round and round as you do with a sauce makes it more likely that the cheese will separate from the liquid).

Once the cheese has begun to melt, return it to a very low heat, stirring continuously. Gradually add the remaining cheese until you have a smooth, thick mass (this takes about 10 minutes, less with practice). If it seems too thick, add some more hot cider. Add the brandy and season with pepper (preferably white, as the grains won't show). Place over your fondue burner and serve with the cubes of bread. Use long fondue forks to dip the bread in, stirring the fondue often to prevent it solidifying. Have wedges of apple on hand to refresh you between mouthfuls of fondue.

What to drink: A dry or medium-dry hard cider will go perfectly.

CHEESE AND SPICY BEAN BURRITOS WITH FRESH TOMATO SALSA

These are lighter than the baked burrito you tend to find in Mexican restaurants. They may look complicated to prepare but you can prepare the beans and salsa ahead of time and put them together at the last minute.

8 oz. queso fresco or other mild, white crumbly cheese

1 large avocado

freshly squeezed juice of 1 lemon or lime

1 tablespoon chopped cilantro leaves

4 large soft wheat tortillas or wraps

½ iceberg lettuce, finely shredded

sea salt and freshly ground black pepper

guacamole and sour cream, to serve (optional)

SPICED BEANS

2 tablespoons olive oil

½ bunch of scallions, trimmed and thinly sliced

2 garlic cloves, crushed

1 teaspoon mild chili powder

1 teaspoon ground cumin

1 large or 2 medium canned tomatoes, plus 2 tablespoons of their juice, or 2 fresh tomatoes, skinned and roughly chopped

14-oz. can kidney beans, drained and rinsed

2 heaping tablespoons chopped cilantro leaves

freshly squeezed lemon juice, to taste

FRESH TOMATO SALSA

1 pint cherry tomatoes

2 scallions, trimmed and thinly sliced

1 green chile, seeded and finely chopped

freshly squeezed juice of 1 lime

2 tablespoons chopped cilantro leaves

SERVES 4

First make the spiced beans. Put the oil in a saucepan over medium heat, then fry the scallions for a couple of minutes. Stir in the garlic, chili powder, and cumin. Add the tomatoes, breaking them up with a spatula or wooden spoon. Tip in the beans, cover with a lid, and cook for about 5–6 minutes until the liquid has evaporated. Take the pan off the heat and mash the beans roughly with a fork. Stir in the cilantro and season with lemon juice and salt to taste. Set aside.

Next make the fresh tomato salsa. Chop up the cherry tomatoes and put them in a bowl with the scallions, chile, and lime juice. Season with salt and stir in the cilantro.

Now get the other ingredients ready. Crumble the cheese. Pit the avocado, then peel and chop the flesh into small cubes, toss with a little lime or lemon juice, season, and stir in the cilantro.

Warm a large skillet over low heat and lay one of the tortillas in the skillet. Let heat up for a minute, then turn it over and heat the other side. Lay it on a board and spread a quarter of the spiced beans in a large square in the middle. Top with a layer of crumbled cheese, then a layer of shredded lettuce. Spoon over a little of the salsa and scatter over a quarter of the avocado. Fold the sides of the tortilla to the middle, then carefully roll the burrito up from the edge nearest to you. Cut across diagonally with a sharp knife and arrange on a plate. Serve with generous servings of guacamole and sour cream, if using, and more of the salsa.

What to drink: I actually enjoy a good lager with a burrito (see page 76) but a glass of Sauvignon Blanc or a dry rosé would also be enjoyable.

IRRESISTIBLE ITALIAN FOUR-CHEESE PIZZA

If, like me, you always reject the pizza "quattro formaggi" as being bland and indigestible, just try making it with top-quality Italian cheeses.

PIZZA DOUGH

1¼ cups bread flour

1 cup cake flour

1 teaspoon fine sea salt

1 envelope quick-acting yeast

½ teaspoon sugar

2 tablespoons olive oil,
plus extra to drizzle

about ¾ cup hand-hot water

semolina or cornmeal,
to dust the baking sheets

PIZZA TOPPING

1⅔ cups homemade* or good-quality,
storebought passata (strained tomatoes)

5 oz. Pecorino Toscano (rind removed),
sliced

5 oz. Taleggio (rind removed) or buffalo
Mozzarella, sliced

3 oz. Gorgonzola piccante, crumbled

⅓ cup freshly grated mature Parmesan

a small handful of fresh oregano
or basil leaves

freshly ground black pepper

2 large baking sheets, lightly oiled

MAKES 2 PIZZAS

To make the pizza dough, sift the 2 flours into a bowl along with the salt, yeast, and sugar. Mix together, then form a hollow in the center. Add the olive oil and half the hand-hot water and stir to incorporate the flour. Gradually add as much of the remaining water as you need to pull the dough together. (It should take most of it—you need a wettish dough.) Turn the dough out onto a board and knead for 10 minutes until smooth and elastic, adding a little extra flour to prevent the dough sticking if necessary. Put the dough into a lightly oiled bowl, cover with plastic wrap, and leave in a warm place until doubled in size, about 1–1¼ hours.

Preheat the oven to 475°F and sprinkle the prepared baking sheets with semolina.

Tip the dough out of the bowl and press down on it to knock out the air. Divide it in half. Pull and shape one piece of dough into a large circle, then place it on a prepared baking sheet and push it out towards the edges of the tray. (It doesn't have to be a perfect circle!) Spread half the passata over the top, then arrange half the cheeses over the top. Season with pepper. Repeat with the other piece of dough and the remaining cheese. Drizzle a little olive oil over the top of each pizza and bake in the preheated oven for 8–10 minutes until the dough has puffed up and the cheese is brown and bubbling. Garnish the pizzas with oregano leaves and drizzle over a little more oil.

* To make homemade passata, heat 2 tablespoons olive oil in a large skillet or wok, add 1 crushed garlic clove, fry for a few seconds, then add 1 level tablespoon tomato paste. Tip in 1 lb. chopped, skinned fresh ripe tomatoes and stir well. Cover with a lid and leave for 5 minutes to soften the tomatoes, then break them down with a fork or wooden spoon. Simmer, uncovered, for a further 5 minutes until the mixture is thick and pulpy. Season with salt, pepper, and a pinch of sugar and let cool. (You can also make this with a 14-oz. can of tomatoes, in which case you won't need the tomato paste.)

What to drink: A fruity Italian red, such as a young Chianti or Rosso di Montepulciano. (Red wine works much better with cooked than uncooked cheese.)

TARTIFLETTE

Tartiflette is a wickedly rich, sensationally good cheese and potato dish from the Savoie region of France. Perfect après-ski/cold weather fare.

2 tablespoons sunflower or other light cooking oil

6½ oz. thick-sliced bacon, diced

2 large onions, thinly sliced (about 14 oz.)

2 large garlic cloves, thinly sliced

1¾ lbs. boiling potatoes, well scrubbed

a sprig of fresh rosemary (optional)

1 small or ½ large Reblochon or other washed-rind cheese (about 9 oz.)

⅔ cup heavy cream

freshly ground black pepper

a large ovenproof dish, buttered

SERVES 6

Heat the oil in a large skillet and fry the bacon until beginning to brown. Remove from the skillet with a slotted spoon. Tip in the onions, stir, and fry over low heat for about 20–25 minutes until they have collapsed right down and are beginning to brown. Add the garlic about 5 minutes before the end of the cooking time. Meanwhile, cut the potatoes, unpeeled, into slices about ⅛ inch thick, place in a saucepan with the sprig of rosemary, if using, and cover with cold water. Bring to a boil and boil for 2 minutes, then remove the rosemary, drain the water, and set the potatoes aside.

Preheat the oven to 400°F.

Cut the Reblochon into thin slices, removing the rind if you prefer. (If you have a very mature cheese with a sticky rind, you may prefer to remove it. I prefer to use a slightly younger cheese and keep the rind, which adds color and texture.)

Tip half the potatoes into the baking dish, cover with half the onions and bacon, and season with pepper. Repeat with the remaining potatoes, onions, and bacon and pour over the cream. Distribute the Reblochon over the top of the dish, then bake in the preheated oven for 15–20 minutes until the cheese is brown and bubbling. Serve with a green salad.

What to drink: A crisp dry wine from Savoie or Switzerland would be ideal with this—the same sort of wine you would drink with a fondue.

LEEK AND BLUE CHEESE QUICHE WITH HAZELNUT CRUST

A good homemade quiche is a wonderful way to enjoy cheese. You can always use a ready-made crust to save time but this nutty crust has a great flavor. If you don't like blue cheese you could easily substitute Cheddar, Gouda, or any other full-flavored cheese. Buy leeks with fresh-looking green leaves rather than those with brown edges.

3 leeks (about 14 oz.)

3 tablespoons butter

3 large eggs

1 cup whipping cream

⅓ cup freshly grated mature Parmesan

3½ oz. medium-strong blue cheese, e.g. Stilton, crumbled

sea salt and freshly ground black pepper

HAZELNUT CRUST

2 tablespoons shelled hazelnuts

⅔ cup all-purpose flour

⅓ cup whole-wheat flour

5 tablespoons chilled butter, cubed

3–4 tablespoons ice water

a deep 9-inch loose-based quiche pan
baking beans

SERVES 4–6

Preheat the oven to 375°F.

First make the crust. Put the hazelnuts on a baking sheet and roast in the preheated oven for 10 minutes or until the skins turn dark brown. (Turn off the oven.) Let cool for a few minutes, then tip them onto a clean kitchen towel and rub off the skins. Transfer to a food processor and pulse until finely chopped but not powdery, then add the flours and pulse once or twice to mix. Add the butter and pulse to incorporate, then add just enough of the ice water to bring the mixture together. Pat the dough into a ball, wrap in plastic wrap, and let rest in the refrigerator for 1 hour.

Meanwhile, trim the bases and cut the coarse outer leaves from the leeks. Thinly slice the leeks and rinse thoroughly to get rid of any dirt or grit. Heat the butter in a large skillet and fry the leeks for 5–6 minutes until beginning to soften. Season well and set aside to cool.

Roll the dough out to a circle big enough to fit your quiche pan. Carefully lower the dough into the pan, pressing it into the edges, and lightly prick the base with a fork. Leave any overhanging dough untrimmed. Refrigerate for 20 minutes. Preheat the oven again to 375°F.

Line the quiche crust with parchment paper, fill with baking beans, and bake in the preheated oven for about 12 minutes. Leave the oven on.

Separate 1 of the eggs, reserve the white, and beat the yolk and the other 2 whole eggs together. Measure the cream in a cup, add the beaten egg and half the Parmesan, season with pepper, and beat well.

Remove the paper and beans from the quiche crust and brush lightly with the reserved egg white. Return to the oven for another 5 minutes, then remove from the oven and reduce the oven temperature to 350°F. Trim the overhanging edge of crust with a sharp knife. Scatter half the blue cheese in the crust, spoon over the leeks, then cover with the remaining blue cheese. Carefully pour the egg and cream mixture evenly over the top (only use as much as you need to fill the crust). Sprinkle over the remaining Parmesan. Bake for about 35–40 minutes until the top is puffed up and lightly browned. Let cool for about 20 minutes before serving. (I personally think it's nicest at room temperature.)

What to drink: Cider is always good with leeks, or a smooth dry white wine like a subtly oaked Chardonnay, a Pinot Blanc, or a Chenin Blanc.

SAFFRON RISOTTO WITH AGED PARMESAN, SAGE, AND SERRANO HAM

A good risotto depends on good ingredients, so make sure you have a well-flavored stock, good-quality ham, and well-aged Parmesan (or Grana Padano) cheese.

2½ cups chicken stock, preferably homemade

3 tablespoons butter

1 small onion or ½ medium onion, finely chopped

1 cup arborio or other Italian risotto rice

½ glass (about ⅓ cup) dry white wine

a Parmesan rind (optional)

a small pinch (about ¼ teaspoon) saffron strands

1–2 tablespoons jellied meat juices* (optional)

¼ cup aged Parmesan, freshly grated, plus a few Parmesan shavings

2 tablespoons olive oil

2–3 slices of Serrano or other Spanish air-dried ham, each torn into 3

8–10 fresh sage leaves

sea salt and freshly ground black pepper

SERVES 2

Bring the stock to a boil, then leave it simmering on a low heat.

Melt 2 tablespoons of the butter over medium heat in a large saucepan, add the onion, and cook gently until soft, about 5 minutes. Tip in the rice, stir, and cook for 2–3 minutes until the grains are opaque and beginning to stick to the bottom of the pan. Add the wine, stir, and let it bubble up and evaporate.

Add the Parmesan rind if you have one, then begin to add the hot stock, adding about a coffee cup at a time and allowing the liquid to be absorbed by the rice before you add the next lot. Cook, stirring regularly, until the rice begins to look creamy but still has some bite to it, about 20 minutes. Pour the last bit of stock over the saffron and add to the risotto along with a couple of spoonfuls of jellied meat juices, if you have some. Turn off the heat, add the remaining butter and the grated Parmesan, and stir. Cover the pan and let the flavors blend for 2–3 minutes.

Heat the oil in a skillet and quickly fry the ham. Remove from the pan with a slotted spoon and drain on a paper towel. Fry the sage leaves in the same skillet until crisp. Give the risotto a final stir, remove the Parmesan rind, and season to taste. Serve in warm, shallow soup bowls and top with the crisp ham, sage leaves, and a few shavings of Parmesan.

* What you want are the umami-rich meat juices that collect under the fat you pour off when you're cooking a chicken or a pork or veal joint.

What to drink: A glass of dry Italian white wine, such as a Soave.

EXTRA-CRISPY MACARONI AND CHEESE

The best bit about macaroni and cheese, as we all know, is the crispy topping, and it suddenly struck me how wonderful it would be to have crispy bits all the way through. It is, and this is how you do it.

4–5 oz. sharp Cheddar, coarsely grated
2 tablespoons butter
3 tablespoons all-purpose flour
1¼ cups whole milk
6 oz. rigatoni or penne
½ teaspoon English mustard or 1 teaspoon Dijon mustard
a few drops of Worcestershire sauce
sea salt and freshly ground black pepper

a shallow ovenproof dish, lightly buttered

SERVES 2–3

Preheat the oven to 325°F.

Sprinkle 1½ oz. of the Cheddar in an even layer over a baking sheet. Bake in the preheated oven for 8–10 minutes until bubbling and beginning to brown. Remove from the oven, let cool, then break into pieces.

Put the butter in a medium nonstick saucepan and melt gently. Stir in the flour and cook for a few seconds, then take the pan off the heat and add the milk little by little, stirring before you add the next amount. Put the pan back on the burner, increase the heat slightly, then bring the sauce gradually to a boil, stirring continuously. Turn the heat right down again and let the sauce simmer for 5 minutes, stirring it occasionally.

Bring a large saucepan of water to a boil, add salt, then tip in the pasta. Cook according to the manufacturer's instructions. Meanwhile, preheat the broiler.

Just before the pasta is ready, stir half the remaining Cheddar into the sauce, add the mustard and Worcestershire sauce, and season to taste. Add a little more milk if it looks too thick.

Drain the pasta thoroughly and tip into the prepared ovenproof dish. Scatter the crispy cheese pieces over the pasta and mix together. Pour in the cheese sauce, then sprinkle over the remaining Cheddar. Place the dish under the hot broiler for about 5 minutes until the top is brown and crispy.

What to drink: A medium-bodied fruity red, such as a Saint-Emilion or other fruity Merlot, works very well.

MAC 'N' GREENS

A healthy spin on macaroni and cheese that can be used as a side for a roast or grilled meat.

3 tablespoons butter
1 medium/large leek, trimmed and thinly sliced
⅓ cup flour
2½ cups lowfat milk
a head of broccoli divided into small florets (about 10 oz. florets)
12 oz. penne (plain or whole-wheat)
2 handfuls of chard or spinach leaves
150 g mature Gruyère
3 heaping tablespoons freshly grated Parmesan
sea salt, freshly ground black pepper, and grated nutmeg

4 or 6 individual ovenproof dishes, lightly buttered

SERVES 4 AS AN ENTREE OR 6 AS A SIDE

Put the butter in a medium nonstick saucepan and melt gently. Add the leeks, stir, and cook for 1 minute, then stir in the flour and cook for a few seconds. Take the pan off the heat and gradually add the milk, stirring continuously. Put the pan back on the burner, increase the heat slightly, then bring the milk gradually up to simmering point. Turn the heat right down again and leave the sauce over very low heat.

Fill a large saucepan with boiling water from the kettle, bring back to a boil, add salt, then add the broccoli and blanch for a couple of minutes. Transfer the broccoli to a strainer with a slotted spoon and rinse with cold water. Tip the pasta into the same water in the pan and cook for the time recommended on the package.

Wash and remove the stalk and central rib from the chard or spinach (unless using baby leaves). Just before the pasta is ready, stir half the Gruyère and the Parmesan into the sauce and check the seasoning, adding salt, pepper, nutmeg, and more Parmesan, if necessary. Add the broccoli and chard or spinach, stir, and set aside for 3–4 minutes. Preheat the broiler.

Drain the pasta and divide between the prepared dishes. Pour over the sauce and vegetables and mix gently, then sprinkle over the remaining Gruyère. Place the dishes on a baking sheet and broil for 5 minutes until the cheese is brown and bubbling.

What to drink: If you're making this as a side for broiled pork or veal, serve a medium-bodied Italian red. An unoaked Chardonnay or Italian white like a Soave would work well with it on its own.

PAGE 119 *Extra-crispy Macaroni and Cheese*
RIGHT *Mac 'n' Greens*

CHARD, ONION, AND PARMESAN GRATIN

You may be tempted to discard the fleshy white central rib of chard leaves but they make a delicate-tasting gratin that can be served as a side vegetable or, with the addition of ham, as an entrée.

1 tablespoon olive oil

2 tablespoons butter

1 medium/large onion, roughly chopped

1 teaspoon finely chopped fresh thyme leaves or ½ teaspoon dried thyme

stalks from a large bunch of chard, washed, trimmed, and sliced, plus 4 chard leaves, roughly shredded

1 tablespoon all-purpose flour

⅔ cup whole milk

1 tablespoon crème fraîche or heavy cream (optional)

⅓ cup freshly grated Grana Padano or Parmesan, plus 3 tablespoons for the topping

2 tablespoons fresh bread crumbs (optional)

sea salt and freshly ground black pepper

a medium ovenproof dish

SERVES 2 AS AN ENTREE OR 4 AS A SIDE

Heat a nonstick saucepan, add the oil and 1 tablespoon of the butter, and tip in the onion. Cover with a lid and cook over low heat for about 5–6 minutes until beginning to soften. Stir in the thyme, then add the chard stalks and cook for another 3–4 minutes. Season. Preheat the broiler.

Stir in the flour, then add the milk, bring to a boil, and simmer until the sauce has thickened. Stir in the chard leaves and cook for 1 minute, then add the crème fraîche and cheese. Tip into the ovenproof dish. Mix the remaining 3 tablespoons cheese with the bread crumbs, if using, and scatter over the gratin. Chop the remaining butter into little pieces and dot over the top. Broil until brown and bubbling.

Variation: You could also add some chopped ham if you wanted to turn this into an entrée dish.

What to drink: If serving this as a vegetable side, be guided by the entrée, otherwise a smooth dry white wine, such as a Chardonnay, will work well.

LEFT *Chard, Onion, and Parmesan Gratin*

MUSHROOM DAUPHINOIS

Adding mushrooms and extra cheese to this gorgeously creamy French potato classic makes it substantial enough to serve on its own, as well as being the perfect accompaniment for roast lamb.

3 tablespoons butter, cubed, plus a little extra for the topping

8 oz. cremini mushrooms, wiped, trimmed, and sliced

1 teaspoon finely chopped fresh thyme leaves (optional)

1¼ cups whipping cream, or 1 cup heavy cream and ¼ cup whole milk

2 garlic cloves, thinly sliced

1¼ lbs. boiling potatoes

½ cup finely grated Gruyère, Beaufort, or Comté

2 tablespoons freshly grated Parmesan

sea salt and freshly ground black pepper

a shallow ovenproof dish, buttered

SERVES 6

Preheat the oven to 375°F.

Heat a large skillet or wok and add the butter. When it has melted and stopped foaming, tip in the mushrooms. Fry for a couple of minutes, then stir-fry until lightly browned. Stir in the thyme and remove from the heat.

Pour the cream into a small saucepan and heat very gently with the garlic. Turn off the heat and let infuse while you peel the potatoes and cut them into very thin slices.

Arrange a layer of potatoes over the bottom of the prepared ovenproof dish. Tip half the mushrooms over the potatoes, sprinkle over half the Gruyère, and season with salt and pepper. Put another layer of potatoes on top, then the remaining mushrooms and Gruyère and season again. Top with the remaining potatoes. Carefully pour over the infused cream, distributing it evenly over the dish. Sprinkle the top with Parmesan. Chop a small slice of butter into little pieces and dot over the top. Bake in the preheated oven for 1 hour–1 hour 15 minutes until the top is browned and the potatoes thoroughly cooked. Let rest for at least 5 minutes before serving.

What to drink: Most medium-bodied reds would work well with this—Pinot Noir would be particularly delicious.

WARM PEAR, GORGONZOLA, AND PECAN TARTLETS WITH MAPLE DRIZZLE

A cheese course and dessert rolled into one—a fabulous finale for a dinner party.

12 oz. ready-rolled puff pastry dough, thawed if frozen
1 egg, lightly beaten
6½ oz. Gorgonzola
¼ cup heavy cream
2–3 ripe pears
½ cup shelled pecans or walnuts
2 tablespoons maple syrup
cayenne pepper

SERVES 6

Preheat the oven to 425°F.

Take the pastry dough out of the refrigerator and let warm up for 10–15 minutes.

Unroll the pastry dough, cut it in half horizontally, then cut each of the halves into 3 to make 6 equal-size pieces. With the tip of a sharp knife, score round each of the squares about ½ inch from the edge to make a border. Lightly brush the border with beaten egg, taking care not to brush over the cut you've made (otherwise the dough won't puff up around the edge of the tartlets).

Put the Gorgonzola in a bowl and break up roughly with a fork, then stir in the cream. Season with a little cayenne pepper and spread over the bases of the tartlets, taking care not to cover the border. Roughly break up the pecans and divide between the tartlets. Peel, core, and quarter the pears, cut each quarter into 3 wedges, and lay them in slices on top of the cheese and nuts. Drizzle a little maple syrup over each tartlet and bake in the preheated oven for 15–20 minutes until the dough is well browned and puffed up. Let cool for 5 minutes before serving.

What to drink: A glass of lightly chilled young tawny port or an Australian Liqueur Muscat would be delicious with these.

LEFT Warm Pear, Gorgonzola, and Pecan Tartlets with Maple Drizzle

LAVENDER HONEY AND VANILLA CHEESECAKE

An extremely easy and delicious cheesecake. If you can't find lavender honey, use any fragrant honey like acacia or orange blossom—or a regular clear honey.

12 oz. fromage frais (not the reduced-fat version)
12 oz. quark or ricotta
2 teaspoons pure vanilla extract
2½ tablespoons raw sugar
3 large eggs, beaten
3 tablespoons lavender honey, acacia honey, or other aromatic clear honey, or to taste

CRUST
5 oz. graham crackers
5 tablespoons butter
1 teaspoon ground cinnamon

an 8-inch loose-based springform cake pan

SERVES 8

Preheat the oven to 300°F. Pour any liquid off the fromage frais and tip into a strainer to drain while you make the base.

To make the crust, put the graham crackers in a plastic bag and crush with a rolling pin until you have even-size crumbs. Melt the butter in a small saucepan, stir in the cinnamon, cook for a few seconds, then stir in the crumbs until they have absorbed all the butter. Tip into the cake pan and distribute evenly. Press down well with the back of a spoon. Place the pan on a baking sheet and bake in the preheated oven for 20 minutes until crisp.

Tip the quark and drained fromage frais into a large bowl. Add the vanilla extract, sugar, and one-third of the eggs and whisk until smooth. Whisk in the remaining eggs. Dip a tablespoon into a mug of boiling water, then add the honey to the cheesecake, a spoonful at a time and dipping the spoon back into the hot water in between each spoonful. Whisk the honey into the cheesecake topping and check for sweetness, adding another spoonful if needed. Pour the mixture onto the crust, put back in the oven, and bake for 30 minutes until just firm. Turn off the oven and let the cheesecake cool, then cover with plastic wrap and refrigerate for at least 2 hours or overnight. Serve with plum, apricot, or rhubarb compote and a dusting of confectioners' sugar.

What to drink: Cheesecake needs a sweet wine with pronounced acidity to offset its richness. A Beerenauslese Chardonnay or a late-harvest Sauvignon Blanc would both work well.

THIS PAGE *Lavender Honey and Vanilla Cheesecake*
RIGHT *Lemon and Blueberry Upside-down Cheesecakes*

LEMON AND BLUEBERRY UPSIDE-DOWN CHEESECAKES

A gorgeous sweet, lemony version of the fashionable French verrine (see page 88) and really easy to make.

3½ oz. graham crackers
5 tablespoons butter
1 teaspoon ground cinnamon
1 cup mascarpone
3–4 tablespoons homemade or storebought lemon curd
2–3 tablespoons lowfat milk
2–3 teaspoons freshly squeezed lemon juice, strained
2 cups fresh or frozen blueberries

a baking pan
4–6 small tumblers

SERVES 4–6

Preheat the oven to 375°F.

Put the graham crackers in a plastic bag and crush with a rolling pin until you have even-size crumbs. (You can do this in a food processor but it tends to make them a bit fine and powdery.) Melt the butter in a small saucepan, stir in the cinnamon, cook for a few seconds, then stir in the crumbs until they have absorbed all the butter. Tip into the baking pan and bake in the preheated oven for 5 minutes until the crumbs are crisp. Set aside to cool.

Tip the mascarpone into a bowl and mix in the lemon curd with a wooden spoon until smooth. (Don't use an electric beater—it will make the mixture seize up and become too buttery.) Add the milk to give a softer, more spoonable consistency and a little lemon juice to adjust the sweetness.

Divide the blueberries between the tumblers. Spoon over the mascarpone mixture and top with the crumbs. Cover the glasses with plastic wrap and refrigerate for an hour or so. (The bases can be made further in advance but don't add the crumble topping too far ahead otherwise it will go soggy.)

* You can vary this idea with other curds and fruits. A raspberry curd and mascarpone mixture, for example, would be delicious with fresh raspberries underneath; a lime curd with chopped kiwi fruit; or an orange curd with mandarin oranges.

What to drink: A late-harvest Riesling would go well with this.

RASPBERRY AND RICOTTA HOTCAKES

This is my spin on what has become a modern classic. They are feather-light, fruity pancakes, perfect for a romantic breakfast or brunch.

1½ cups fresh or part-thawed raspberries
3 tablespoons sugar
½ cup ricotta
2 eggs, separated
⅓ cup whole milk
½ cup all-purpose flour
½ teaspoon baking powder
a pinch of salt
2 tablespoons butter
crème fraîche or heavy cream, to serve (optional)

SERVES 2–4 (DEPENDING HOW HUNGRY OR GREEDY YOU ARE)

Set aside ⅓ cup of the raspberries and put the remainder in a small saucepan with 2 tablespoons of the sugar. Set over low heat and leave until the sugar has melted and the raspberries start to bubble up. (Add a little more water if necessary.) Set aside.

Put the ricotta in a bowl with the remaining sugar and the egg yolks, beat together with a wooden spoon, then mix in the milk. Sift the flour, baking powder, and salt into the ricotta mixture and stir in.

Gently melt the butter in a small saucepan over low heat.

Whisk the egg whites in a clean bowl with an electric handheld whisk until stiff. Fold a heaping tablespoon of the egg whites into the ricotta mixture to loosen it. Lightly fold in the remaining egg whites and the raspberries you've set aside.

Heat a skillet, pour in a little of the melted butter, then drop 2–3 tablespoons of the batter into the skillet. Let the hotcake cook for a couple of minutes over low heat, then carefully turn it over with a palette knife and cook the other side. Cook the remaining hotcakes in the same way, adding a little more butter to the skillet each time. Hand the hotcakes out straightaway with the warm raspberry sauce and a bowl of crème fraîche or a small pitcher of heavy cream (not that it needs it but it's extra-delicious this way!)

What to drink: Delicious with a cappuccino for breakfast or with a glass of Prosecco for a brunch.

RIGHT Raspberry and Ricotta Hotcakes

PARMESAN AND BACON SCONES

These light, airy little scones are so easy to rustle up and make a delicious snack.

2 slices of fatty bacon, rinded and finely chopped
1¾ cups self-rising flour
2 teaspoons baking powder
¼ teaspoon salt
a pinch of cayenne pepper
¼ cup freshly grated mature Parmesan
3 tablespoons chilled butter, cubed
1 egg, plus enough lowfat milk to make ⅔ cup liquid
extra milk, to glaze (optional)
cream cheese or mascarpone, to serve

a 2-inch cookie cutter
a large baking sheet, lightly oiled and dusted with flour

SERVES 4

Preheat the oven to 425°F.

Heat a skillet and fry the bacon over moderate heat until crisp. Set aside to cool.

Sift the flour, baking powder, salt, and cayenne pepper into a large bowl. Rub in the butter with your fingertips, keeping the mixture as light as possible. Stir in the Parmesan and bacon.

Make a well in the center and pour in most of the egg and milk mixture, pulling the mixture together as you go. Add just enough egg mixture to bring everything together into a dough, then stop. (You can do all this in a food processor, if you like.) Turn the dough out onto a lightly floured work surface and lightly press it into a rough circle about 1 inch thick. Stamp out the scones with your cookie cutter, pressing the offcuts of dough lightly together to make the last few scones. Brush the scones lightly with milk or the remaining egg and milk mixture and put on the prepared baking sheet. Bake in the preheated oven for 15 minutes until well risen and lightly browned. Turn out onto a wire rack to cool completely. To serve, split and spread with cream cheese or mascarpone.

DOUBLE CHEESE AND BACON MUFFINS

These irresistibly gooey, cheesy muffins are very simple to make—you just need to take care not to overmix them.

4 slices of bacon, very finely chopped
1 onion, finely chopped
7 tablespoons butter, cubed
2½ cups all-purpose flour
1 tablespoon baking powder
½ teaspoon salt
2 heaping tablespoons plain yogurt
about ½ cup whole milk
3 eggs, lightly beaten
¼ cup freshly grated mature Parmesan, plus a little extra for the topping
3 oz. sharp Cheddar, diced

a nonstick muffin pan with 12 deep holes or a regular muffin pan lined with nonstick paper cases

MAKES 12 LARGE MUFFINS

Heat a skillet and fry the bacon until the fat begins to run. Add the onion and continue to cook over low heat until the onion is lightly browned. Set aside and let cool.

Gently melt the butter in a small saucepan over low heat.

Preheat the oven to 375°F.

Sif the flour, baking powder, and salt into a large bowl, then sift it again and make a well in the center. Put the yogurt in a large measuring cup and mix in enough milk to make up a scant cup.

Pour the melted butter, eggs, and yogurt and milk mixture into the flour along with the Parmesan. Mix in lightly and swiftly with a large metal spoon to create a rough batter. (This should only take a few seconds—do not overmix otherwise the finished muffins will be tough.) Fold in the bacon, onion, and Cheddar. Spoon the batter into the holes or paper cases in the muffin pan and sprinkle with a little more Parmesan. Bake in the preheated oven for about 25–30 minutes or until fully risen and well browned. Leave in the pan for 5 minutes, then transfer to a wire rack for another 10–15 minutes to cool slightly. Eat warm with soup or a salad.

LEFT *Parmesan and Bacon Scones*

TOASTED SEED AND FENNEL BREAD

Toasted seeds, especially fennel seeds, are particularly good with cheese, so try incorporating them into this easy, tasty bread.

2 tablespoons fennel seeds

2 cups bread flour, plus a little extra to dust

1¼ cups whole-wheat flour

¾ cup rye flour

1½ teaspoons quick-acting yeast

1½ teaspoons fine sea salt

⅓ cup mixed toasted seeds, plus extra to sprinkle

1 tablespoon malt extract

1⅓ cups hand-hot water

2 tablespoons sunflower or canola oil

a baking sheet, lightly oiled

MAKES 1 MEDIUM LOAF

Warm the fennel seeds over low heat in a dry skillet until they begin to change color and yield their fragrance. Let cool.

Mix together the flours in a large bowl. Stir in the yeast, salt, and mixed toasted seeds, including the fennel seeds. Dissolve the malt extract in 2 tablespoons of the hand-hot water. Make a well in the center of the flour and pour in the malt extract and water, the sunflower oil, and the rest of the water. Start working the flour into the liquid with a wooden spoon, then mix with your hands until all the flour is incorporated.

Turn the dough out onto a lightly floured work surface and knead for 7–8 minutes until the dough begins to feel elastic. Place the dough in a large bowl covered with a clean, dampened kitchen towel and leave for about 45–50 minutes until doubled in size.

Tip the dough out of the bowl and press down on it to knock out the air. Roll up the dough into a long oval, tucking in the ends to neaten the shape. Place on the prepared baking sheet, make 4 diagonal cuts in the top with a sharp knife, cover with the kitchen towel, and leave for another 25 minutes. Meanwhile, preheat the oven to 400°F.

Brush the top of the loaf lightly with water and sprinkle a couple of tablespoons of mixed toasted seeds over it. Bake in the preheated oven for about 35–40 minutes until the loaf is well browned and sounds hollow when you tap it on the base. Let cool on a wire rack for a good 45 minutes before serving.

QUICK ZUCCHINI, FETA, AND MINT BREAD

Quick, flavored breads like this are hugely popular in France where they refer to them as "cake." In fact, they're more like a cross between a quiche and a bread, nice to serve with a bowl of soup or cut into cubes as a pre-dinner nibble with a glass of wine.

2 tablespoons butter

4 scallions, trimmed and thinly sliced

10 oz. zucchini, trimmed and coarsely grated

2 tablespoons finely chopped fresh mint leaves

1½ cups all-purpose flour

1 tablespoon baking powder

3 large eggs, beaten

6 tablespoons lowfat milk

6 tablespoons light olive oil

5 oz. Feta, crumbled into small pieces

sea salt and freshly ground black pepper

*a 9 x 4-inch nonstick loaf pan,
lightly oiled and dusted with flour*

SERVES 6

Preheat the oven to 350°F.

Heat a large skillet or wok and add the butter. When it has melted and stopped foaming, tip in the scallions and zucchini. Stir-fry over high heat for 1 minute, then remove from the heat and stir in the mint. Let cool for 20 minutes, then strain off any excess liquid.

Sift the flour and baking powder into a bowl and season well. Whisk the eggs, milk, and oil in another bowl, then tip two-thirds of it into the flour. Beat well, then add the remaining egg mixture. Mix in the Feta and fried scallions and zucchini, then transfer to the prepared loaf pan. Bake in the preheated oven for 50 minutes or until a skewer inserted in the middle comes out clean. Let cool, then remove from the pan. If not serving immediately, wrap in foil and store in the refrigerator. Serve at room temperature, sliced and cut into halves or squares.

What to drink: A glass of crisp Sauvignon Blanc, such as a Sancerre, would go particularly well with this.

RIGHT *Toasted Seed and Fennel Bread*

TALEGGIO AND GRAPE FOCACCIA

This gorgeously gooey bread makes a great accompaniment for a selection of antipasti.

2 cups bread flour

2 cups cake flour

1 teaspoon quick-acting yeast

1 teaspoon raw sugar

2 teaspoons fine sea salt

1¼ cups hand-hot water

2–3 tablespoons olive oil,
plus extra to drizzle

⅓ cup freshly grated Parmesan

6 oz. Taleggio (rind removed), thinly sliced

2½ oz. Gorgonzola, thinly sliced

5 oz. red seedless grapes

2 sprigs of fresh rosemary, torn into pieces

a little fine or coarse semolina (optional)

coarse sea salt and freshly ground
black pepper

*a 7 x 13-inch baking pan, lightly greased and
dusted with fine semolina, if using*

SERVES 6–8

Put the flours, yeast, sugar, and salt in a large bowl. Mix well, then make a well in the center. Pour in the hand-hot water and 1 tablespoon of the olive oil, then bring the mixture together, first with a wooden spoon and then with your hands. Add a little extra water, if necessary. Tip the dough out onto a lightly floured work surface and knead until smooth and it springs back when you press it with a finger, about 5–6 minutes. Put in a lightly oiled bowl, cover with plastic wrap, and let rise for about 45 minutes or until doubled in size.

Tip the dough out of the bowl and press down on it to knock out the air. Give it a couple of swift turns on the work surface, then divide in half but make one half slightly bigger than the other. Stretch and press the larger of the 2 halves into the prepared baking pan so that it covers the base and comes up the sides. Sprinkle over the Parmesan, then add the sliced Taleggio and Gorgonzola and cover with the grapes. Season well with pepper. Roll out and stretch the other piece of dough to fit over the filling, bringing up the dough underneath and pressing to seal round the sides. Cover with plastic wrap or a kitchen towel and leave for another 30 minutes or so to rise.

Fifteen minutes before you think the dough will be ready, preheat the oven to 425°F.

Using the tips of your fingers, make deep indentations in the dough, taking care not to deflate the whole bread, and push the rosemary into the holes. Brush the surface with the remaining olive oil and season with coarse salt. Bake in the preheated oven for 10 minutes, then reduce the heat to 400°F and cook for another 15 minutes until the bread is well risen and golden. Drizzle with a little more olive oil, let cool for 5–10 minutes, then cut into squares or strips.

CHEDDAR AND CRACKED PEPPER STRAWS

Cheese straws are a great way to use up the last bits and pieces of hard cheese, particularly a good sharp Cheddar.

1 cup plus 2 tablespoons all-purpose flour

¼ teaspoon English mustard powder

a pinch of sea salt

6½ tablespoons chilled unsalted butter, cubed

5 oz. sharp farmstead Cheddar, grated

2 tablespoons coarsely ground black pepper

1 egg yolk

1–2 baking sheets, lightly oiled

SERVES 6–8

Sift the flour, mustard powder, and salt into a bowl. Cut in the butter and rub together with your fingertips as if you were making pastry. Add the Cheddar and pepper and rub in thoroughly. Beat the egg yolk with 2 tablespoons water and add just enough of this mixture to the flour to enable you to pull it together into a dough. Shape into a flat disk, wrap in plastic wrap, and refrigerate for 30 minutes, then take out and let come back to room temperature.

Preheat the oven to 375°F.

Roll out the dough thinly, then cut into strips about 12 inches long. (Don't cut off the uneven ends—that's what makes them look homemade!) Lay the strips carefully on the prepared baking sheets and bake in the preheated oven for 12–15 minutes until golden brown. Leave on the trays for 10 minutes, then carefully transfer to a wire rack to finish cooling. Eat fresh, ideally, but they will keep well for a couple of days in an airtight container (you can refresh them briefly in a warm oven).

OAT CRACKERS FOR CHEESE

I came across these in a London restaurant, The Greenhouse, which prides itself on its cheese board. Chef Antonin Bonnet created them to complement a wide range of cheeses, a task it very successfully fulfils.

1¾ cups all-purpose flour

⅓ cup buckwheat flour

½ teaspoon baking soda

1½ teaspoons fine sea salt

¼ teaspoon finely ground white or black pepper

2 sticks softened butter, cubed

3 egg whites

1¼ cups rolled oats

cookie cutters in different sizes
several baking sheets lined with nonstick parchment paper

MAKES ABOUT 45 CRACKERS

Sift the flours, baking soda, salt, and pepper into a bowl. Put the butter and egg whites in a food processor and whizz until smooth. Add half the flour mixture and pulse to blend, then the remaining flour and finally the oats. (If your processor isn't big enough, tip the mixture into a large bowl once you've added the first lot of flour and add the rest of the flour and the oats by hand). Form the dough into a flat disk, wrap in plastic wrap, and let rest in the refrigerator for at least 1 hour.

Preheat the oven to 375°F.

Divide the dough into 4. Roll each quarter out thinly and stamp out rounds with the cutters (I like to make these in different sizes). Transfer carefully to the prepared baking sheets and bake in the preheated oven for 12–15 minutes until lightly colored and crisp.

LABNEH WITH HERBS, RAW VEGETABLES, AND FLATBREAD

Cheese is surprisingly easy to make. This is a Middle Eastern version that simply requires some yogurt, salt, and cheesecloth. Depending on how long you let the cheese drain, you can create a soft, spreadable, dunkable cheese or a slightly firmer one that you can roll into balls. Either makes a stylish and unusual light meal.

two 16-oz. containers full-fat plain yogurt
1 scant teaspoon fine sea salt

TO SERVE
extra virgin olive oil
2 heaping tablespoons chopped fresh flatleaf parsley, cilantro, and mint leaves
strips of raw carrot, cucumber, and celery
black and green olives
Sardinian crisp flatbread and warm pitta bread strips

a large square of cheesecloth
kitchen twine

SERVES 4–6

Lay the square of cheesecloth over a large bowl. Mix together the yogurt and salt, then tip carefully into the lined bowl. Pull the edges of the cheesecloth square together and tie securely with kitchen twine to form a bundle. Hang over the bowl or the sink and leave for about 12–16 hours.

If using straightaway, tip the drained cheese from the cheesecloth into a bowl and make a shallow dip in the center. Drizzle over some olive oil, scatter with the chopped herbs, and serve with the raw vegetables, olives, and flatbread. If eating it later, you can store it in the refrigerator in a covered bowl or box for up to 36 hours.

* If you don't want to make this labneh from scratch, you can get a similar result by mixing 2 parts plain yogurt to 1 part cream cheese.

LABNEH BALLS WITH DUKKAH

You can roll these easy labneh balls in homemade dukkah or the same freshly chopped herbs used to serve the Labneh (left). You could also preserve them, uncoated, in a jar of olive oil in the same way as the Feta recipe opposite.

1 recipe Labneh (see left)

DUKKAH
1 cup whole, skinned almonds or a mixture of almonds and hazelnuts
2 tablespoons coriander seeds
1 tablespoon cumin seeds
½ cup sesame seeds
1 teaspoon sea salt
½ teaspoon black peppercorns
1 teaspoon dried oregano

MAKES ABOUT 8 OZ.

Prepare the labneh following the recipe on the left, but let drain for an extra 12 hours or so until firm. Roll the thoroughly drained cheese into walnut-size balls.

To make the dukkah, preheat the oven to 350°F.

Spread the almonds (and hazelnuts, if using) and coriander, cumin, and sesame seeds separately on baking sheets or in baking pans. Roast in the preheated oven until lightly colored and fragrant—about 7–8 minutes for the nuts, 5 minutes for the coriander seeds, 4 minutes for the cumin seeds, and 3–4 minutes for the sesame seeds. Set aside and let cool.

With a mortar and pestle, grind together the sea salt with the peppercorns and oregano. If you feel energetic, you can grind the coriander and cumin seeds too (you'll need to do this in batches).

Chop the almonds (and hazelnuts) roughly, then tip them into a food processor. Pulse to break them up, then add the sesame seeds and coriander and cumin seeds, if you haven't already ground them. Process again until you have a roughly textured mixture that looks like coarse bread crumbs. Add the oregano mix and pulse once to blend. Store in an airtight container.

Roll the labneh balls in the dukkah or alternatively in mixed, chopped fresh herbs as suggested above.

PAGE 139 *Labneh with olive oil, olives, and flatleaf parsley*

MARINATED FETA WITH HERBS

You can buy Feta ready-marinated but if you do it yourself it will look and taste much better.

2 bay leaves
a few sprigs of fresh thyme and rosemary
1 thin strip of lemon or orange zest
6½ oz. Feta, cut into large cubes
1 teaspoon mixed or black peppercorns, lightly crushed
1–2 dried chiles (optional)
2 cups extra virgin olive oil

1–2 wide-necked preserving jars, sterilized (see page 4)

SERVES 3–4

Put the bay leaves, thyme, rosemary, and lemon zest in a small saucepan of boiling water and blanch for 30 seconds. Remove with a slotted spoon and set aside to cool.

Layer the Feta cubes in the preserving jar(s), tucking the herbs, lemon zest, peppercorns, and chiles between them. Pour over enough olive oil to cover the cheese completely. Put a lid on the jar(s) and store in the refrigerator for 2–3 days. Bring to room temperature before serving and use within 2 weeks.

* For a quicker result, you can marinate Feta in olive oil and a little lemon juice and flavor it with chopped fresh mint or dried oregano and finely chopped chile, but it won't keep.

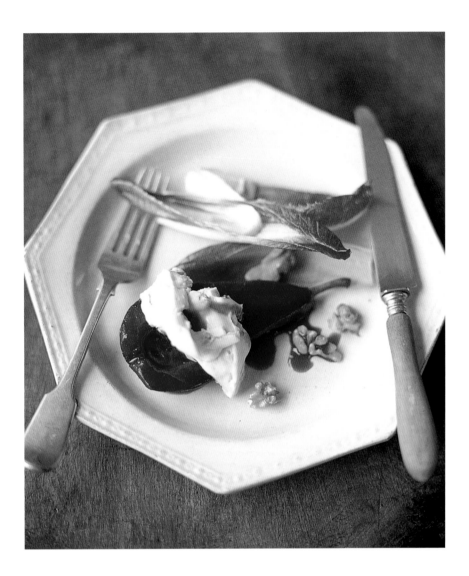

PEARS IN PINOT NOIR

Poached pears (or plums) in red wine make a delicious accompaniment for a creamy blue cheese.

3 pears
½ cup packed light brown sugar
(depending how ripe and fruity the wine is)
1½ cups inexpensive Pinot Noir
1 piece of cinnamon stick or star anise
3 cloves
balsamic vinegar, to taste (optional)

SERVES 6

Peel, halve, and core the pears (leave the stalk on for decoration). Put the halves in a saucepan with the sugar, wine, and enough water to cover, then add the cinnamon and cloves. Bring slowly to a boil until the sugar dissolves, then reduce the heat and simmer for about 40 minutes or until the pears are tender.

Taste the pear syrup and add a few drops of balsamic vinegar if necessary to correct any excessive sweetness. Let cool.

Make up a dessert plate with a few bitter salad greens, such as radicchio, a generous scoop of soft blue cheese, such as Gorgonzola dolce, a few toasted walnuts, and a little of the syrup spooned over the top.

GRAPE JELLIES

These are an attractive alternative to plain grapes.

1 teaspoon powdered gelatin
1¼ cups red grape juice
10 oz. red or black seedless grapes

6 small glasses or shot glasses

SERVES 6

Sprinkle the gelatin in a shallow dish with 2 tablespoons cold water. Let dissolve for 2–3 minutes. Meanwhile, gently heat the grape juice in a small saucepan until almost boiling. When the gelatin has dissolved, pour it into the grape juice, stir, then let cool.

When the jelly is cold, wash the grapes, halving the larger ones. Fill the glasses with the grapes, then top up with the jelly. Cover with plastic wrap, put in the refrigerator, and let set, pressing the fruit down into the jelly halfway through the setting time.

See picture on page 142.

GEWURZTRAMINER JELLY CUBES

Gewurztraminer has an exotic flavor that makes a great accompaniment for washed-rinded cheeses like Munster. For a striking effect, make it into a jelly.

1 packet powdered gelatin
2¼ cups Gewurztraminer
2–3 tablespoons sugar syrup

SERVES 6–8

Sprinkle the gelatin in a shallow dish with 3 tablespoons cold water. Let dissolve for 3 minutes. Meanwhile, gently heat the Gewurztraminer in a small saucepan until almost boiling. When the gelatin has dissolved, pour it into the warm Gewurztraminer. Remove from the heat and stir until well blended. Sweeten the liquid jelly to taste with the sugar syrup. Pour the jelly into a shallow rectangular tin, cover, and put in the refrigerator to set for 2 hours.

Cut the jelly into cubes with a sharp knife and serve with cheese.

SPICED QUINCE COMPOTE WITH RED WINE AND CLOVES

Quinces turn a beautiful jewel-red color when they are cooked—making this compote a lovely accompaniment for a mellow blue cheese, such as Stilton or Jasper Hill Farm's Bartlett Blue.

2 large or 3 smaller quince
a good squeeze of lemon (about 1 tablespoon)
6 tablespoons raw sugar
1 cinnamon stick
6 cloves
1 thin strip of orange zest (optional)
1 cup fruity red wine

SERVES 8–10

Peel, core, and quarter the quince, then cut into even-size dice. (This is tougher than it sounds—quince are very hard!) As you cut them, put them in a saucepan of acidulated water (i.e. water with a good squeeze of lemon juice) to stop them discoloring.

When you've finished chopping, drain off the water, add the sugar, cinnamon, cloves, and orange zest, if using, pour over the red wine, and top up with water to cover. Set the pan over low heat and cook, stirring occasionally, until the sugar has dissolved. Bring the syrup up to boiling point, then reduce the heat, half-cover the pan, and simmer until the quince is soft (up to 1 hour). You may need to top up the liquid with boiling water so that the quince always remain covered.

Remove the cooked quince pieces from the pan with a slotted spoon and transfer to a bowl. Continue simmering the syrup until it is thick and coats the back of a spoon. Strain it onto the quince, let cool, and then serve. The compote can be stored in a lidded container in the refrigerator for up to 1 week.

* You could play around with the spices in this recipe and add 6 lightly crushed cardamom pods or 2 pieces of star anise instead of the cloves.

LEFTOVER CHEESE

If you have relatively small leftover pieces of cheese, it's better to find some use for them in the kitchen than to store them—see page 151. And there are many tasty options, from cheese on toast (page 69) to pizza toppings (page 111).

You obviously need to check that the cheese is still edible and within its expiration date, if it has one. A bit of mold on a hard cheese isn't necessarily a problem (it can be trimmed off) but discard cheeses that have developed brownish patches or that smell in any way unpleasant. And don't take any risks at all if you or the person you're serving it to is pregnant or elderly (see page 4).

My favorite use for leftover bits and pieces is an incredibly easy-to-make cheese spread which the French call "fromage fort" ("strong cheese"). Simply whizz a couple of cloves of garlic in a food processor, add your sliced-up cheese (having first removed the rinds), and pulse until you have a thick paste. Add just enough white wine to make a spreadable consistency and season with cayenne pepper or ground chile to taste. For an even stronger version, you could use a splash of eau de vie or brandy. The spread will keep in the refrigerator for 2–3 days and makes a tasty topping for crackers, crostini, or toast. Here are two other simple recipes for leftover cheese.

WELSH RAREBIT

3 tablespoons full-bodied English ale

½ cup grated sharp Cheddar

1½ teaspoons all-purpose flour, sifted

1 egg yolk

¼ teaspoon English mustard

½ teaspoon Worcestershire sauce

1 large or 2 smaller slices of sourdough or country bread

freshly ground black pepper

SERVES 1

Preheat the broiler.

Pour the ale into a saucepan, sprinkle over the Cheddar and flour, and stir. Cook over low heat until the cheese has melted and you have a smooth sauce. Remove from the heat and beat in the egg yolk, then add the mustard and Worcestershire sauce. Season with plenty of pepper (you shouldn't need salt).

Broil or toast the bread, then spread with the melted cheese and broil until brown and bubbling.

STILTON AND PARSLEY BUTTER

7 tablespoons unsalted butter, at room temperature

3½ oz. Stilton (weighed with the rind removed)

1 heaping tablespoon finely chopped fresh parsley

sea salt and freshly ground black pepper

SERVES 8–10

Cut the butter and cheese into small chunks. Place in a bowl and beat together (this is easiest with an electric handheld whisk but you can use a wooden spoon). Season generously with pepper and a pinch of salt and mix in the chopped parsley. Spoon the flavored butter onto a piece of foil, shaping it into a rectangle. Roll the foil around the cheese to create a cylinder, then twist both ends of the foil and refrigerate until firm.

Remove from the refrigerator about 20 minutes before serving. It's particularly good with hamburgers or steak.

RIGHT *Welsh Rarebit*

CHEESE KNOW-HOW

Finn

HOW TO BUY CHEESE

Although most supermarkets sell an impressive range of cheese these days, and there are some excellent online sites (see page 158), in my view there's nothing to beat buying from a specialist store or market stall where you can taste the cheese and even talk to the producer.

In fact with handmade, artisanal cheese, I would say it's always preferable to buy this way because it changes so much from batch to batch and from season to season. And even a cheese you think you like can be disappointing if it's not been properly looked after—a hazard in some stores that don't rotate their stock sufficiently regularly.

A good store by contrast may well perform the role of an *affineur* (see page 13), bringing their own cheeses to peak condition. If you shop there regularly, they get to know your tastes and introduce you to new cheeses you might enjoy. The assistants will be able to explain where the cheeses come from, what milk they're made from, and what style of cheese they are. They will always cut off a sliver for you to try. They can suggest other cheeses and accompaniments that will complement it or, if you're cooking with it, advise which will work best in the recipe you're planning. The whole experience is a delight, the only downside being the temptation to buy more than you really need or can use before they deteriorate. ("Little and often" or "buy as you need it" is by far the best counsel when you're buying artisanal cheese.)

The advantage of buying in supermarkets is that quality control is paramount. They're very good at sourcing the popular cheeses like Monterey Jack, Cheddar, and Stilton, where their huge buying power secures them some of the best of what's available. And they can afford—or twist the producer's arm—to offer them at keener prices than independent stores.

Buying direct from the producer is fun too. I regularly buy from a cheese maker in south-west England who takes a stall at my local farmers' market. He specializes in goat cheese and has some I often buy but I am always amazed at how they vary from batch to batch and season to season. He also experiments with new cheeses, which are always worth trying.

Finally, there's the internet—again tempting—with the online suppliers' wide selection of cheeses and detailed, knowledgeable descriptions. Many of the top cheese shops now have an on-line presence, a boon if you live far from a specialist store. But packaging and transport costs can make them an expensive option.

ORDERING CHEESE IN A RESTAURANT

Ordering cheese in a restaurant can be intimidating, especially if they trundle around a huge cheese cart for your inspection, often with cheeses you've never heard of before. Usually a "cheese sommelier" will run through the options but sometimes there are so many that you forget what they all are. The best way to handle the situation, I find, is to make clear the type of cheeses you prefer and ask which of their cheeses are new, seasonal, or locally produced. That way, you taste varieties of cheese you might not have tried before.

SERVING TEMPERATURES

Possibly the most important piece of advice in this book is to bring your cheese to cool room temperature before serving it.

Eating cheese straight from the refrigerator dumbs down its taste and means that you lose around 50 percent of its flavor. Small cheeses will take a shorter time than whole ones or large pieces of cut cheese. Allow at least 45 minutes and up to 2 hours.

Don't on the other hand let cheese get too warm otherwise it will accentuate its fat content and develop an unpleasantly "sweaty" consistency—a potential problem during unseasonally hot weather or when you're eating alfresco (see page 71).

CHEESE TIP

Don't rule out a style of cheese on the basis of one example you've tried and disliked. Cheeses vary hugely in strength. Even the most pungent washed-rind cheeses and blues have milder versions you might enjoy and there are many goat cheeses that are not remotely "goaty." Do keep tasting and trying!

CHEESE KNIVES AND BOARDS

A lot of specialist knives are sold for cutting cheese these days. You could theoretically have a different cutter for every type of cheese and indeed some purists do recommend this so that you keep the flavor of each cheese apart. Most of us, however, would settle for two or three knives at most, one round-bladed one for softer cheeses, a sharper one for harder ones, and possibly an extra knife for any particularly pungent cheese. I also find a cheese slicer useful for sandwiches.

If you're serving or plating up cheese from the kitchen, you can use ordinary kitchen cutlery. I actually like the effect of using a less than perfectly sharp knife. I don't want my cheese in immaculately straight lines. A couple of dessertspoons are useful for scooping an oval lozenge of soft cheese onto a plate, while a fork will break up a hard cheese into attractively irregular pieces to scatter over a salad. An ordinary vegetable peeler is also useful for getting finer shavings than you can achieve with a purpose-designed cheese slicer.

Other than small round cheeses, which it makes sense to cut into wedges, I don't buy into the idea that cheese should be cut in certain specified ways. People get quite upset if you cut straight across the end of a slice of **Brie**, for example. If that matters to you, I suggest slicing the cheese just before you bring it to the table. That can actually make your cheese board look quite striking, although there is the disadvantage that any unused cheese will dry out more quickly.

The one type of presentation I don't think looks particularly attractive is cutting cheese into cubes or batons. It's hard to do anything else with a block cheese but it rather underlines the fact that your cheese is factory-made rather than artisanal. Maybe that smacks of cheese snobbery but I like cheese to look as natural as possible. Hard cheeses also taste better when they're finely sliced or shaved, rather than chopped, so that they can almost dissolve on the tongue.

SHOULD YOU REMOVE THE RIND?

I wouldn't remove the rind before serving the cheese course. If the rind is a feature of the cheese, as it is in a washed-rind cheese or a crusted blue like **Stilton**, for example, I would always present it like that at the table, even though my guests might then want to remove it. Indeed I recommend that you do remove the rind once the cheese is on your plate if you think it will interfere with the accompanying wine you're drinking—see page 30.

CHEESE BOARDS

I like to vary the way I serve cheese depending on the selection. A rustic board can look great with traditional cheeses, such as **Camembert**, **Cheddar**, and **Stilton**, but sometimes you can create a more striking effect with a slate (especially with white and white-rinded cheeses), marble, or other surfaces (see page 52). A shallow basket lined with vine leaves can also be attractive.

STORING CHEESE

Cheese is an expensive product so if you're to get the best out of your investment, you need to take care of it once you get it home and plan how you're going to use it. It's too easy to consign it to the fridge and then forget about it.

Store cheese in the warmer part of the refrigerator (at the top if there isn't a freezer compartment or in an empty salad drawer) as soon as you buy it.

Once cheese is unwrapped it will deteriorate more quickly. At the end of a meal, wrap any remaining cheese and put it away as soon as possible, as it dries out quite easily. Ideally, use waxed paper but if you don't have that, use parchment paper for soft cheese, foil for blues, and plastic wrap for harder cheese. Each cheese can then be put into a sealable bag to stop them transmitting and picking up flavors from other ingredients. Very strong-smelling cheeses may need to be wrapped in a damp kitchen towel and enclosed in a plastic box to prevent their smell pervading the fridge! If you do keep cut cheeses any length of time, you should rewrap them every couple of days.

As a general guide, hard cheeses, whole cheeses, and larger pieces of cheese stay fresher longer than soft ones, cut ones, and small pieces. And commercial and pasteurized ones keep better than unpasteurized, artisanal ones.

CAN YOU FREEZE CHEESE?

Purists would say no—the flavor will be affected—but they will be fine for cooking. Mature cheeses tend to freeze better than young cheeses with a high water content, such as **goat cheese**.

CHEESE AND HEALTH

Cheese is a healthy food which contains elements that are an essential part of a balanced diet. You might think that that goes without saying but the idea has got about that cheese is somehow unhealthy either because of the amount of fat it contains, because some people have difficulty tolerating certain cheeses, or because of the pasteurization issue.

I'll touch on these issues below and opposite but let's concentrate on the positives first of all. Cheese is a source of protein, which, as you probably don't need me to tell you, is vital for cell renewal and repair and to keep our bodies functioning healthily; calcium, which is essential for bone and dental health; and essential vitamins, such as A, B12, and D, which assist with good vision, a stable mood, and the absorption of calcium respectively.

It's the quantity of cheese you eat that can have deleterious effects. If you're a compulsive snacker, you will certainly put on weight, as you can see opposite, but modest portions (and just 1 oz. **Cheddar** provides 216 mg calcium) can do nothing but good.

IS UNPASTEURIZED CHEESE SAFE?

Many of the world's most coveted cheeses are unpasteurized, i.e. made with raw, untreated milk (see page 13). Most of us have no problem with that but if you're pregnant or elderly, the advice is that you should avoid unpasteurized cheeses.

WHAT IF I'M PREGNANT?

In addition to unpasteurized cheeses, the current view is that uncooked, mold-ripened cheeses, such as **Brie**, **Camembert**, and some **goats' cheeses** and **blue cheeses**, should be avoided, as they carry a higher risk of listeria, a bacteria that can be harmful both to the unborn child and anyone with a compromised immune system.

WHAT IF I'M VEGETARIAN?

Many cheeses are made by adding rennet, an animal-derived substance that comes from the stomachs of calves, which curdles the milk and separates it into curds and whey (see page 11). However, producers often use a similar enzyme from nonanimal sources. Cheeses are usually clearly labelled as suitable for vegetarians but if you're unsure, always check with the retailer or cheese producer. Vegans do not eat any animal-derived products so don't offer cheese to a vegan guest.

WHAT IF I CAN'T TOLERATE COW'S MILK?

People who have a lactose intolerance find that they suffer from bloating, cramps, and other symptoms after eating cheese, particularly cow's milk cheese. They lack enough of the enzyme lactase, which breaks down lactose and makes it digestible.

They may find they can eat cheese from other animals, such as sheep, goats, and buffalo but these contain lactose too so consult your guests first.

CUTTING YOUR CHEESE CALORIES

However delicious, cheese is a calorific food. There's no getting away from it, but it's more often the other foods you eat with it that add up to the calorie overload. Bread, cookies, butter, potatoes, pasta, and cream—all the yummy things in life, unfortunately—pile on the pounds if you don't exercise some portion control!

The good news is that there are less indulgent ways to enjoy cheese and that some cheeses are less calorific than others, most notably younger, fresher cheeses that have a higher water content. The list below shows the number of calories per 3½ oz. but bear in mind that a recommended portion size is generally less than a third of that (see below) and that individual cheese recipes vary (artisanal cheeses, for example, tend to be higher in calories than commercial versions).

There are also low-calorie versions of higher-calorie cheeses but I'm never particularly impressed with them. I would always rather enjoy the full-strength versions and eat slightly less of them.

LOWFAT CHEESES (PER 3½ OZ.)

Young, soft cheeses
Cottage cheese: 114 calories
Lowfat fromage frais: 50 calories
Fresh goat cheese: 160 calories (but goat cheese logs are higher in calories)
Quark: 66 calories
Ricotta: 134 calories

MEDIUM-FAT CHEESES (PER 3½ OZ.)

White-rinded and Greek cheeses
Brie: 296 calories
Camembert: 283 calories
Feta: 262 calories
Halloumi: 315 calories
Mozzarella: 274 calories

HIGHER-FAT CHEESES (PER 3½ OZ.)

Hard cheeses and those with added cream
Sharp Cheddar: 416 calories
Gruyère: 409 calories
Pecorino: 397 calories
Stilton: 412 calories
Mascarpone: 435 calories
Parmesan: 401 calories

A LOWFAT CHEESE AND ONION DIP

To make a lowfat cheese dip, use **quark**, one of the lowest-calorie cheeses on the market with about 66 calories per 3½ oz. Mix a 9-oz. tub with about ½ cup lowfat or skim milk to create a smooth, dipping consistency. Add ½ small onion, very finely chopped, a crushed garlic clove, ½ teaspoon sea salt, and a dash of Tabasco green pepper sauce.

WATCH YOUR PORTION SIZE!

As you can see, it's not so much that all cheese is highly calorific, rather it's the amount of it we eat. It's also worth keeping consumption in check because cheese is high in saturated fats.

On most weight-control programs, a recommended portion for a hard cheese is 1 oz. and slightly more (1½ oz.) for a soft, lower-fat cheese. That might not sound a lot but it will seem more generous if you cut or shave it finely, grate it, or crumble it, rather than serving it as a single piece.

CUTTING YOUR CARBS

Another strategy is to cut out (or reduce) any accompanying carbohydrates in the form of bread or crackers. The French typically eat their cheese on its own when they're having it during a meal (a picnic is another matter when the customary baguette is a must!)

If you can't do without, there are now many elegant alternatives to the rather spartan crispbreads that used to be the rule: lowfat, seed-topped flatbreads and crisp Sardinian *carta da musica* being two of my favorites. And think in terms of open Scandinavian-style sandwiches rather than the normal double-sided ones (see page 75). Even for a party you can hand round canapés based on fruits and vegetables rather than bread, cracker, or pastry bases or serve them on cocktail sticks. Here are some ideas using lowfat cheeses.

◆ Sticks of celery filled with tarragon-flavored **quark**
◆ Thick slices of cucumber topped with **quark** or **fromage frais** and smoked salmon (you can adapt the ideas for the verrines on page 88)
◆ Cherry tomatoes, split and filled with **lowfat soft cheese**, flavored with a dash of Tabasco
◆ Watermelon and **Feta** kabobs
◆ Greek salad on a stick: a cube of **Feta**, a cherry tomato, a square of cucumber, and a black olive
◆ Halved fresh figs topped with creamy **blue cheese**

QUICK CHEESE AND WINE MATCHER

As you will have already seen, there are many alternative suggestions for drink pairings in the section on What to Drink with Cheese (see pages 28–47) but if you're looking for a match for a specific cheese, here's a brief summary to make your task quicker. Do remember though that the age and condition of the cheese and the accompaniments you pair with it will make a difference.

Appenzeller: Swiss white wines, schnapps

Beaufort: Wines from the Savoie region of France, dry amontillado sherry, aged tawny port, bière ambrée

Brie: Soft fruity reds, such as cru Beaujolais and Pinot Noir, fruity rosés, raspberry- and cherry-flavored beers, Guignolet, Japanese plum wine

Brillat-Savarin: Champagne and other sparkling wine, apricot brandy

Cabrales: sweet oloroso sherry, Bual and Malmsey Madeira, Malaga

Caerphilly: Cava or still Xarel-lo, Gavi di Gavi, English Bacchus, Côtes du Rhone

Camembert: Cider, Pommeau, Calvados, Oregon or New Zealand Pinot Noir

Cantal: Port, Rhône reds such as Gigondas and Chateauneuf du Pape, Biere de garde

Cashel Blue: *See* Stilton. You could also try an Irish malt whiskey.

Chaource: Chablis and Champagne

Cheddar: Vintage port, medium-dry hard cider, English ales, oak-aged beers, barrel-aged Chardonnay, sherry cask-aged whiskey

Cheshire: red Bordeaux, Bergerac, hard cider, apple juice

Comté: Vin jaune, dry amontillado sherry, white Bordeaux

Epoisses: Sauternes, strong Belgian beers, Marc de Bourgogne or Marc de Champagne, Genever

Feta: Greek white wines, such as Assyrtiko, ouzo

Fourme d'Ambert: "Porty" reds, such as Zinfandel, Negroamaro, Bandol, port

Gaperon: Crisp dry whites, and simple rustic French reds, such as Marcillac

Goat cheese: Sauvignon Blanc is the outstanding match. German Kabinett or dry Alsace Riesling, witbier, apple schnapps, and elderflower cordial are all good.

Gorgonzola: Passito di Pantelleria, Vin Santo, Amarone

Gouda: Tempranillo-based reds, Argentine Malbec, dry amontillado sherry, tawny port

Gruyère: Amontillado and dry oloroso sherry, 20-year-old tawny port, smoked beer, sake

Humboldt Fog: Sauvignon Blanc or dry rosé

LEFT *(From top) Gorgonzola, Perroche, Manchego (from left to right: 6, 7–9, 9–12, and 14 months old)*

Manchego and other hard sheep's cheeses: Rioja and other Tempranillo-based reds, Roussanne and Marsanne-based whites, fino sherry, dry madeira, quince-flavored liqueurs, sake

Maroilles: Trappist beers, such as Chimay Bleue, eaux de vie

Mimolette: Red Bordeaux and other Cabernet-Merlot blends

Morbier: Spanish reds, such as Rioja

Mozzarella: Rarely eaten without accompanying ingredients, usually tomato. Best served with dry Italian whites or, as a pizza topping, with fruity Italian reds.

Munster: Gewurztraminer, sweet Alsace or German Riesling, plum-flavored eaux de vie, and Belgian and Northern French beers

Ossau-Iraty: South-western French and Languedoc reds, such as Madiran and Corbières. Dry southern French or Spanish rosé, bières ambrées, and dry hard cider.

Parmesan (Parmigiano-Reggiano): Classic, medium-bodied reds, such as Bordeaux and Chianti, Champagne and similar sparkling wines, Maury, and Banyuls

Pecorino: Italian reds, Poire William

Pont-l'Evêque: Sparkling hard cider, Pommeau, Calvados or other apple brandies, aromatic whites, such as Alsace Pinot Gris

Reblochon: Pinot Gris from Alsace, Trappist beers, marc

Roquefort: Sauternes and similar sweet Bordeaux, peaty Islay whiskies, such as Lagavulin

St George: Dry Riesling, Chardonnay, or Sancerre. Also Cabernet Sauvignon.

Stilton/Stichelton: Sweet red wines, such as port, elderberry wine, sloe gin, tawny port, sweet sherry, Tokaji, barley wines, peaty whiskies, mead

Stinking Bishop: Strong apple or pear aperitifs and digestifs, hard cider, and barley wine

Taleggio: Franciacorta sparkling wine, Arneis, Grüner Veltliner, Barbera

Tête de Moine: Rich, oak-aged Chardonnay, Côtes de Rhône Villages, amber ales, dry, nutty sherries

Tomme de Savoie: Crisp, dry whites from the Savoie region, dry Riesling

Torta del Casar: Aged Rioja, Cava Reserva

Vacherin Mont d'Or: Champagne (especially vintage Champagne), crisp dry whites from Switzerland and the Savoie region of France

Valençay: Loire whites, such as Quincy, Menetou-Salon, and Sancerre (or other mineral, cool-climate Sauvignon Blancs), mature Alsace Riesling

Wensleydale: Wheat beer, and Côtes du Rhone

CHEESE GLOSSARY

Cheese aficionados tend to use a special vocabulary which can sometimes be confusing to ordinary mortals. Here's what they're talking about:

Affineur: Literally a "cheese maturer"— a craftsman who takes cheeses from a producer and brings them to perfect maturity (see page 13). They usually have their own shops.

Aged cheese: Cheeses that are deliberately matured to develop their flavor. Parmesan and Gruyère are common examples. Sometimes referred to as "cave-aged," simply meaning this process has been carried out in a cellar.

Alpine cheese: Synonym for the semihard cheeses that are made in the Alpine regions of France Switzerland and Italy, such as Gruyère, Emmental, and the various tommes and tomas. A broader description than "Swiss cheese," which refers more specifically to Emmental-style cheeses.

Artisanal cheese: A handmade cheese made on a farm or by a small producer from locally sourced milk.

Block cheese: Industrially produced hard cheeses produced in large

amounts. The shape may be uninspiring but the flavor can be perfectly good.

Bloomy-rinded: The sort of white, velvety rind you find on cheeses, such as Brie and Camembert and some goat cheeses. Also known as white-rinded.

Curds: The solid portion of the milk that remains when it is separated from the liquid whey following the addition of rennet or other coagulant (see page 11).

Dutch cheese: Gouda or Gouda-style cheeses (see page 21)

Farmstead cheese: Rather loosely used as a marketing term but should strictly refer to cheeses that have been produced on a farm by the owner of the animals in question.

Fresh: Fresh as in young, rather than fresh as opposed to stale. Commonly used of soft, unrinded, spreadable cheeses, especially young goat and sheep's cheeses.

Mold: Sounds unappetizing but does not necessarily mean moldy. The mold may have been deliberately introduced to develop the flavor of the cheese as in a blue cheese (see page 22).

Mold-ripened: Another description for bloomy-rinded cheeses. such as Brie and Camembert.

Natural-rinded: Natural-rinded cheeses are those which develop a rind simply by being exposed to the air. (Unlike washed-rind cheeses, the rind is not washed or treated.) In practice, this term is mainly used of goat cheeses that have been allowed to mature and develop a grayish, wrinkled rind. As the cheese becomes dryer, the flavor becomes more intense. The French cheese Crottin de Chavignol is a good example.

Paste: The center of the cheese, inside the rind casing.

Pasteurized: Cheese that has been heat-treated to prevent bacterial growth.

Raw-milk cheese: Unpasteurized cheese made from untreated milk.

Rind: The surface that develops over a matured cheese which may be hard, "bloomy" (see above), or slightly sticky, as in a washed-rind cheese.

Semihard cheese: Confusingly used in different ways by different experts. Some consider any cheese which is not well aged and crumbly like a Parmesan to be "semihard" and would categorize Cheddar this way. Others—including me —use the term to refer to cheeses, such as Gruyère and Gouda, that are firm but still have some pliability.

Semisoft cheese: Cheeses that are sliceable but which have a flexible, bendable consistency. Most washed-rind cheeses, such as Munster and Reblochon, are semisoft, as are Camembert and Brie, although they are seldom described this way.

Swiss cheese: General description for Emmental-style cheeses that have holes in the paste.

Washed-rind cheese: Cheeses whose surface is washed or rubbed with a salt water solution or with wine, beer, cider, or marc to develop their flavor, e.g. Epoisses and Stinking Bishop.

TASTING TERMS

Barnyardy/Farmyardy: Terms often used of a well matured, washed-rind cheese, for obvious reasons.

Buttery: Often used of creamy cow's milk cheeses, such as Brillat-Savarin or Explorateur.

Citrussy: The fresh, light notes you tend to find in young goat cheeses and delicately flavored cheeses, such as Chaource.

Fruity: The complex flavors you tend to find in Alpine cheese, such as Comté and Beaufort, which reflect the flavors of the floral- and herb-rich pastures on which the animals graze.

Mushroomy: A term often used of Brie and similar cheeses which can often taste of raw mushrooms.

Nutty: Used of aged cheeses, such as Cheddar, Gouda, and Gruyère.

Piquant: Used of cheeses that have a pronounced savory sharpness or "bite," such as aged Parmesan.

Pungent: An alternative word for strong (and occasionally stinky).

Ripe: A cheese that has reached its peak of flavor (usually after careful maturation).

Sharp: A positive attribute in a cheese, indicating well-defined flavors. Often used of Cheddar and blues, such as Roquefort.

Stinky: *See* Barnyardy.

Strong: A cheese with a more pronounced flavor than is typical of its type, as in a "strong" Cheddar.

ABOVE (From left) Double Gloucester, buffalo Mozzarella, Parmesan, aged Pecorino, Colston Bassett Stilton, cheese grater, Strachitunt, button of goat cheese (top), and Charolais goat cheese (below)

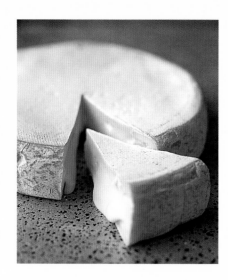

CHEESE SUPPLIERS AND WEBSITES

US

Artisanal
2 Park Avenue
New York, NY 10016
Telephone: 212-725-8585
Brilliant New York cheese shop and bistro, fizzing with great ideas for enjoying cheese. Terrific website too.
www.artisanalcheese.com
And www.artisanalbistro.com

Cowgirl Creamery
Cowgirl Creamery at Tomales Bay Foods
80 4th Street
Point Reyes Station, California
Telephone: 415-663-9335
Exuberant California-based cheese producers and retailers.
www.cowgirlcreamery.com

Dean & Deluca
Several locations
Telephone: 800-221-7714
Purveyor of fine food and kitchenware, including excellent cheese shop.
www.deandeluca.com

Murray's
254 Bleecker Street
New York, NY 10014
Telephone: 212-243-3289
New York's other great cheese shop. Runs a great program of cheese courses.
www.murrayscheese.com

Zabar's
2245 Broadway
New York, NY 10024
Telephone: 212-787-2000
Long-established New York food emporium with a fine cheese counter.
www.zabars.com

FRANCE

Bernard Antony
Superb Alsace-based cheese affineur, supplier to many of France's 3-star Michelin restaurants.
http://pagesperso-orange.fr/fromagerieantony/Fromager.htm

Fromages.com
French-based, English language website with a large selection of French cheeses.
www.fromages.com

Marie-Anne Cantin
Top Parisian affineur and cheese shop.
www.cantin.fr

Rodolphe Le Menier (Tours)
Innovative affineur and cheese shop.
www.fromages-en-jazz.com

FOR MORE INFORMATION

The Cheeselover
My regular cheese blog!
http://thecheeselover.blogspot.com

American Cheese Society
Main organization representing American cheese makers and retailers.
www.cheesesociety.org

British Cheese Board
Promotional body for British cheese.
www.britishcheese.com

French Cheese
An A–Z of French cheeses.
www.frencheese.co.uk

Specialist Cheesemakers Association
Comprehensive listing of British-based cheese makers and shops.
www.specialistcheesemakers.co.uk

Australian Specialist Cheesemakers' Association
A similar site for Australian cheeses.
www.australiancheese.org

FOR COOKWARE

Crate & Barrel
www.crateandbarrel.com
Telephone: 800-967-6696

Sur La Table
www.surlatable.com
Telephone: 800-243-0852

Williams-Sonoma
www.williams-sonoma.com
Telephone: 877-812-6235

The publisher would like to thank **Summerill & Bishop** for the kind loan of the glass domes on pages 2–3. Visit their shop at:
100 Portland Road
London W11 4LN
Telephone: 44 (0)20 7221 4566
www.summerillandbishop.com

INDEX

CONVERSION CHARTS

Weights and measures have been rounded up or down slightly to make measuring easier.

Volume equivalents:

American	Metric	Imperial
1 teaspoon	5 ml	
1 tablespoon	15 ml	
¼ cup	60 ml	2 fl.oz.
⅓ cup	75 ml	2½ fl.oz.
½ cup	125 ml	4 fl.oz.
⅔ cup	150 ml	5 fl.oz. (¼ pint)
¾ cup	175 ml	6 fl.oz.
1 cup	250 ml	8 fl.oz.

Weight equivalents:		Measurements:	
Imperial	Metric	Inches	Cm
1 oz.	25 g	¼ inch	5 mm
2 oz.	50 g	½ inch	1 cm
3 oz.	75 g	¾ inch	1.5 cm
4 oz.	125 g	1 inch	2.5 cm
5 oz.	150 g	2 inches	5 cm
6 oz.	175 g	3 inches	7 cm
7 oz.	200 g	4 inches	10 cm
8 oz. (½ lb.)	250 g	5 inches	12 cm
9 oz.	275 g	6 inches	15 cm
10 oz.	300 g	7 inches	18 cm
11 oz.	325 g	8 inches	20 cm
12 oz.	375 g	9 inches	23 cm
13 oz.	400 g	10 inches	25 cm
14 oz.	425 g	11 inches	28 cm
15 oz.	475 g	12 inches	30 cm
16 oz. (1 lb.)	500 g		
2 lbs.	1 kg		

1 stick of butter = 8 tablespoons = 120 g

Oven temperatures:

110°C	(225°F)	Gas ¼
120°C	(250°F)	Gas ½
140°C	(275°F)	Gas 1
150°C	(300°F)	Gas 2
160°C	(325°F)	Gas 3
180°C	(350°F)	Gas 4
190°C	(375°F)	Gas 5
200°C	(400°F)	Gas 6
220°C	(425°F)	Gas 7
230°C	(450°F)	Gas 8
240°C	(475°F)	Gas 9